All inquiries should be addressed to:
Easy Money Press
5419 87th Street
Lubbock, TX 79424

Revised edition - ISBN 1-929714-01-7
-First printing 2003
-Second printing 2005

First edition published as - ISBN 0-9654563-0-7

Manufactured in the United States of America

How To Pad Your Expense Report... And Get Away With It!

by Employee X

Ea$y
Money
Pre$$

Notice of Disclaimer

The material in this book is meant purely for informational and entertainment value, and is not an endorsement to purchasers or readers in any way.

The author and publisher of this book cannot be held responsible for the acts committed by purchasers or readers, nor the resulting disciplinary action an employer may take against any person who chooses to act upon any of the information contained in this book.

-Easy Money Press

How To Pad Your Expense Report... And Get Away With It!

by Employee X

Table of Contents

Chapter One

Introduction & Disclaimer

<u>WARNING!</u>
If you are and want to remain a pure and honest soul, without so much as a tarnish on your record, DO NOT READ ANY FURTHER! Exposure to the following material will forever change your life.

I'm not setting myself up to be father confessor, nor am I setting myself up to be the devil, tempting you with lucre in order to snatch your immortal soul. What I am willing to do, is show you hundreds of ways to either enhance the legitimate rewards which come along with having an expense account, or increase, legitimate or not, the amounts for which you are reimbursed.

You have to search your own soul and conscience to decide how many of these techniques you wish to use, and how far you are willing to push the limits. You can tell I am writing under a pen name. Obviously, if one of my current superiors were to read this book, they would audit every expense report I've ever submitted.

I am a high level manager within a Fortune 500 corporation. For the past twenty years of my thirty-two work years, I've worked for two prominent companies. In each, I've used almost everything I'm sharing with you in this book.

Knock on wood, I've never been caught. From time to time, someone will question a particular entry on an expense report, but so far they have easily been explained using one of the many excuses I will also share with you.

Read the whole book and take time to consider everything you will read. If you elect to use some of these techniques, I can not be responsible for the results. Don't blame me if you get caught and lose your job. Don't blame me if you have to go to church and confess your sins every week. Don't blame me for the several thousands of extra dollars in your pocket.

What's In It For You?

All you have to consider, is basic math. Let's say you submit only ten dollars a week in bogus or inflated expenses. That is $520 a year in found money to you.

Better yet, this money is, by law, tax free. By the rules of the IRS, legitimate business expenses incurred by an employee in the course of normal business, are reimbursed without impacting that employee's taxable status. In other words, it is not income. In theory, there is no net benefit to the employee.

The principles in this book are contrary to these rules. If you only spend $200, but collect $300 from your employer from a padded expense report, you're getting $100 in extra income. If the IRS knew about it, they'd want to tax it. Do us all a favor and don't tell them.

If you live in a tax bracket, like most middle class people, where the government takes about 40 percent of your money to redistribute the wealth, your $520 of extra expenses, equals more like $870 of gross income.

In fact, by the time you consider social security tax, Medicare tax, state disability tax, and other local taxes; there's a lot of you out there losing fifty cents on the dollar to the government. So, every extra dollar you can get paid on an expense report to you, actually means two dollars in your pocket.

Now look at the multiple. If you're in a position where you could average $100 a week in false expenses, you boost your take home income by $5200 a year, which is a pre-tax pay raise of $8700.

And if you are one of those executives (I know at least one of you is reading this) who could hide $500 a week in extra expenses, the net cash in your pocket is about $26,000, which means you unilaterally gave yourself at least a $43,000 raise.

I don't know about you, but I could always find some use for a few extra bucks for free. Just remember, this is in addition to all of the legitimate perks expense accounts can bring you. With the frequent flyer miles, the free nights in hotels, the meals for yourself and friends, and free legal and financial advice you get, your actual income is significantly larger than the gross number you see on your personal check stub.

How Do I Justify It?

Actually, I've been doing it and getting away with it for so long, I don't even worry about it any more. Most of the little tricks I will teach you have become second nature, it feels natural. If you are going to do this, they better become second nature to you. The more natural these become, the more believable you will appear on the rare occasions you are asked to explain what you did.

When I do worry about it though, I first look at all of the profits my company makes and the cruel things they are willing to do to make them. If the company needs to make their bottom line by laying off a hundred workers, you can bet they don't lose any sleep over it. They are not concerned with the kids whose fathers or mothers no longer have jobs.

Second, I look at some of the obscene salaries the executives make. How is it that in a year where a car company loses a billion dollars, the CEO gets a million dollar bonus? How is it that an airline can ask for pay concessions from their workers to make ends meet, and then have the board of directors fly to the Bahamas for a meeting where they vote themselves a big pay raise? They watch out for their own, so why shouldn't I?

Third, what most workers do not know, are the perks upper management give to themselves. They aren't written down anywhere. They're just one of those "oh by the way" kind of things. Usually they begin at the vice-president level. They give themselves the small privilege of using one of the company cars, or exclusive use of a company health club, or memberships at golf courses, or season tickets to professional sports. When there are stock options to pass around, they take the lion's share and pass along the meager remains to be shared by the next level of management. They justify it using my fourth reason.

I am salaried, which means I get the same amount of money every week in my paycheck regardless of how many hours I work. This normally is an attractive thought, in that you dream you can come in at nine and leave at four, except for Wednesday afternoon when you golf. That only works for the elite in the corporation. You find they want you to work longer hours for the same dollars.

When you are salaried, you first find you are asked to fly on Sunday so you are there for a Monday morning meeting. You are asked to give up a Saturday so the company can reduce airfare with the Saturday night stay. When the company has to have someone stay late for some project, you get to stay because they would have to pay overtime to the hourly workers. To the company, you are free, read in "slave", labor.

All of the personal time you spend flying for the company, spending nights on the road in hotels, and all of the driving time you spend behind the wheel is lost time. Padding your expenses to get a few extra bucks, is still a bargain for the company and some meager compensation to you.

I don't want to sound bitter, but one thing I have found out the hard way, is that you are expendable if it suits the company's needs. The company, and the on going existence of the key executives, comes first.

Have you ever wondered what really goes on in a corporate merger? It's a lot like sand lot baseball games. One of the two company leaders gets their thumb on the knob of the bat. They will pick the first corporate officer who gets to stay with the company. Then the other CEO picks their choice, and so on down the line. I assume I'm the uncoordinated, myopic geek who is going to be picked last.

As the fecal material runs down the hill, each level of management asks, "Who can I give the shaft to, to save my butt." They got and are still getting "theirs", and they will protect it at all costs. I know if it protects their position, they will dump me like a hot potato , so I figure, I'm going to get my part of the pie while I can.

I've been "down sized" twce in my career and it isn't fun. You give years of dedicated service to your company, without any black marks on your record and plenty of successes to note. One day, your company determines the little box on the organizational chart with your name in it, is no longer needed.

Your boss calls you in and hands you an already prepared check and tells you, "I'm sorry, it's nothing personal, but you're being laid off. You've done great work for us and it's a shame, but that's life in the big corporate world."

In further discussions, you find out it really has nothing to do with you or the job you've done. They needed the reduction in head count, and your box is expendable. No discussion of other areas for you to work, just good bye.

Well, I'm sorry too. It's nothing personal, but if I can be kicked out the door for doing nothing wrong, why should I worry about a few extra bucks taken from the company's coffers?

The Business Philosophy of Expenses

This may sound crazy to some of you, but businesses actually want expenses. Granted, they do not want too many of them, but they need them. In some business situations, particularly sales, your superiors may even think you are not doing your job if you don't spend enough on entertaining.

The old "three martini lunch" is what makes the business world go round. It may have been replaced with alfalfa sprout sandwiches and mineral water, but the business lunch charged to somebody's company is the oil which keeps the gears of industry turning.

The reasoning is actually the same one used to justify padding your expense report. Depending on how a corporation is structured, their tax brackets can be higher than yours. The difference is corporations pay taxes on "profits" not income.

Legitimate business expenses are "offsets" against profits. Every dollar spent on expenses hides a dollar of profits from the IRS. Therefore, every dollar they spend on legitimate expenses gains them fifty cents of invisible profits.

This logic is most often used by accountants in what is called the accrual method of bookkeeping. At the end of each month, quarter, or year the company accrues for "anticipated" expenses which may or may not actually show up next quarter.

If the company gets toward the end of the year and there looks as if there is going to be a tax liability, they will accrue as many "probable" expenses as they can. Anything which looks like it might be paid in the next year, will be "accrued" this year, so that on paper they owe less in taxes.

If these expenses never actually materialize, they'll just wait until next year's results to see what to do. Officially, accountants use this to "level" the ups and down of the fiscal roller-coaster. At strategic times, it is used to confuse the tax collectors.

In most of my jobs I have been encouraged to spend the company 's money. I spent a few years as a Sales Manager, controlling the efforts of fifteen sales reps. If I wasn't buying dinners and paying for golf outings for customers, my boss would actually walk into my office and ask, "What the hell aren't you doing out there?"

My boss actual feared the "other guys" in town were buying everyone better lunches, so if we didn't, we'd lose the business. My boss thought competitors were giving away more and better gifts than I was.

The same thing trickled down to my sales reps. I had two who were equally successful, over-achieving their goals by about the same percentage. One had huge expense reports every week, with golf outings at least once a week and lunches almost every day. The other would have one tenth the amount of expenses.

Mind you, both were hammering their numbers by similar amounts, and logic would make you think, "If I can have the same revenues coming in for one tenth the amount of expenses, that is a good thing." Not in the business world. My boss examined the expenses for sales reps and her impression was the first rep was being "more active and involved", and received more praise and awards that the latter. Go figure.

Record Keeping and Your Boss's Oversight

The real secret of padding your expense report and getting away with it is documentation. Actually, the more accurate word would be over documentation. The more information you provide, the more legitimate your report will appear.

People normally think being vague and hoping your boss will overlook the expense, is the best method, as it leaves you more "wiggle room" when it comes time to explain. They think that falling back upon "I can't remember" will work all of the time. It doesn't work.

Just think about it. If you can never remember important details, how intelligent are you? If you can't remember who you had lunch with, how can they trust you with real responsibility?

Stand by your expenses proudly and confidently. Your boss is less likely to question them. If the boss does ask, explain them calmly and definitely. Put your boss on the spot by saying something like, "Did I not understand the expense policy correctly?"

The fact is, your boss doesn't want to spend a lot of time reading and approving expense reports. Okay, so there are a few anal retentive types out there who use a microscope to examine reports, but they are rare.

Most bosses will spend less than thirty seconds auditing an expense report. Most actually rely on their secretaries or administrative assistants. An executive making sixty dollars and hour, can't waste ten minutes ($10) to find a three dollar discrepancy. Multiply this by however many reports they deal with on a weekly basis, and they really don't want to bother.

The secretary is a much softer touch. First, most secretaries or administrative assistants, don't like the way they are treated by their boss, so having to do the "boss's work" by auditing reports, is not one of their favorite tasks either.

Most secretaries are underpaid and overworked. They usually only have time to see if each item is backed by a receipt. If there is a receipt for each entry and an explanation for the expense which seems reasonable, they'll approve it or tell the boss to approve it without being questioned.

You can help your chances if you are nice to the secretary. If you know they are a primary auditor, offer to help them out. Spend a few minutes to ask, "Am I providing you everything you need on those expense reports? Is there anything I can do to make it easier for you to process my expense report?"

Thank the secretary for turning the reports around quickly. You tell them, "These business expenses make my charge card bills build up so fast, and your processing my reports quickly helps keep me out of a financial bind. I'm sure you can sympathize."

The secretary sees your expenses and most likely is amazed you can handle them. Most business expenses would severely impact most secretaries on what they're paid. What you really are saying to her though is, "Thanks for not looking too closely at my expenses."

As another hint, it really wouldn't hurt to buy the secretary lunch (Hide it on your expense report?) or buy them a little gift some time for the hard work they are doing to help you with expense reports. A little bit of goodwill can buy a big amount of leeway.

I'll cover much of the documentation issues within subsequent chapters and where they will more directly pertain to situations. It is important, however, to realize the key piece of documentation is the receipt. Receipts come in all shapes and sizes. Receipts can be obtained from many sources and in many ways, not necessarily by actually incurring the expense.

The local office supply store needs to become your friend. The warehouse type of office supplier can become your very best friend. Businesses buy receipt materials somewhere. Can you guess where? You got it. The office supply store.

The basic restaurant order books with the tear-off receipt at the bottom are available in pads of fifty, ten pads to the package for less than ten bucks. They are available in many designs, colors, and sizes. If you buy a few different kinds, you'll have a lifetime supply of receipts.

A word of warning here though. Most all of them have serial numbers at the bottom for internal controls by the restaurant. Make sure you rotate randomly through the numbers. Sequential receipt numbers on an expense report would be a dead give away.

Mastercard and Visa slips are also available in various formats at the office supplier. Depending upon how sophisticated you want to be, imprinting machines can be bought, and the imprint plates can be ordered. In most states, no proof of an actual business is required to order a plate for the imprinting machine.

You might be asking yourself, "What about those electronic charge card printers? Don't they prevent you from doing this?" I have two things to say about them.

First, sometimes they break down and store clerks have to resort to the old manual method. So, if you want to use hand written receipts once in awhile, that would be your excuse.

Second, running adding machine tape through the printer of a personal computer can produce literally hundreds of types and styles of official looking receipts, complete with logos if you like. Just copy the formats of some you've actually seen.

In fact, there are a number of very small printers available for personal computers designed specifically for labels and receipts. They are cheap. You can buy one with the software to run it for less than $150 new. If you buy someone's used one, you'll spend less than $50.

Your personal computer can be the best forger of documents you could ever ask for. Disks of clip art are available for all of the major corporations around the country. Their logos are on them. Many smaller town hotels still print their receipts on plain old blank paper. The cost of a printer for your PC is less than $100.

If you want real blank invoices from hotels, you can get some in at least three ways. The first would be to ask for it. Tell the clerk, "I just love the format of your receipts. I'm sure my bosses would like to see if it would work for our company. Could I have a few blank sheets to show them?"

Often, loading their printers or a by-product of producing invoices all day, many blank pages result and are kept by the clerks for use as scratch paper. If you see blank invoices lying around, act a bit flustered and ask, "I need a piece of scratch paper, can I have one of those blank invoices there?"

Of course, there is the old stand-by of looking in the trash basket. Typically, the late shift cleans out the baskets for the day shift and places the bags of trash out for the morning janitor to pick up. They are typically in easy reach and seldom watched.

More details about receipts later.

Your Company's Rules to Watch

Some companies have been writing new expense policies to close many of the loop-holes and prevent their employees from cheating on their expense reports. In most cases, their act of closing one hole opens another even larger hole. Nonetheless, the first step in padding your expenses and getting away with it, is to understand all of the rules.

Per Diems

From the Latin for "per day", this is a blanket fixed dollar amount designed to cover all your expenses. Companies do not require you to turn in a receipt for these. In fact the whole idea behind a company using per diems for expenses is to reduce paperwork and lower the time spent by supervisors examining expense reports - just what we need.

If the employee spends more than the per diem, it is their loss. If the employee spends less, they get to keep the difference, ostensibly to cover overages on other days. The less money you spend, the more money you keep. If there ever was a time to be cheap, this is it.

The IRS has established standards for the amounts paid, based on area of the country in which you are traveling and type of per diem your company pays. Most companies claim they are paying the IRS approved amount, but most do not, or they choose to pay the lowest, regardless of the area in which you are traveling. Go to the library and look up the rules.

If you find they are not paying the correct amount, challenge your company to update their per diem amounts to be in "compliance" with the IRS. If they won't, you may be able to recapture the difference on your personal income tax.

Simple per diems start with incidental expenses. A company may pay all travel, lodging, and meals for an employee and then offer them a small fee ($10) per day to cover all other expenses such as laundry and tips while on site.

The most complicated per diems are designed to cover all travel, lodging, and meal expenses and can be quite large. You see these mostly in the sales arena and in particular with what are called "independent" sales reps. In some cases and areas, this could be hundreds of dollars per day.

The most commonly used per diem is meant to cover meals and incidentals. The company pays actual expenses such as airfare, hotels, and rental cars, and then expects the employee to manage the per diem to cover everything else. This type of per diem, according to IRS guidelines, varies as to the part of the country traveled, but ranges between $25 and $50.

If you have the more complicated, all inclusive per diem, you're already probably enough of a skin-flint that you know how much you can economize to make extra bucks, so I'll limit my comments to the simpler, more typical one for meals and incidentals.

Economizing is the key to pocketing as much of the per diem as possible. Choose a hotel which serves a free breakfast. Take a couple of pieces of fruit with you to eat during the day, and you can most likely skip lunch. Some hotels also have evening "happy hours" with free hors d'oeuvres, which often are enough for a meal.

If you want to eat on the cheap, try the grand openings of grocery stores or hardware stores. They often have 25 cent hot-dogs and free drinks. Find the restaurants with all you can eat buffets. Lunches here are usually a couple bucks cheaper than dinner for the same items. Eating a big, later lunch could allow you to skip dinner.

Of course, any time anyone wants to buy you lunch or dinner, let them. Even if they're a salesperson. Better to have a free meal and listen to a sales pitch you don't want to hear, than to pay for your own meal out of your per diem.

Stay at hotels which have a mini or full kitchen and fix your own meals. They are always cheaper and often healthier than restaurants. Just having a refrigerator in your room can save you big dollars on your per diem.

Never ask a bellperson to carry your bag if your are strong enough. Don't tip them unless they really did you a service, particularly if you wanted to carry your own bag but they insisted to do it themselves. Better to be snubbed by the bell clerk than to throw good money away. Check your baggage inside the airport terminal. Don't pay the sky cap to do what the airlines will do for free.

If parking, while on the road, is part of your per diem, find some free parking instead of using the hotel's garage. Better to walk a block or so, then to lose a few bucks a day.

If parking, back home at the airport, would be part of your per diem, ask friends or your spouse to drive you to the airport and pick you up. If you have none, check to see if a cab ride back and forth to the airport is cheaper than the rate you'd pay at the parking garages.

Charge Card Receipts vs. Tear Off Tabs

In situations where the expense policy pays for individual meals, some companies have tried to prevent submissions of the typical tear off restaurant receipt, by requiring you to turn in the actual charge card slip. I've already discussed a couple of ways around this.

The company policy typically reads something like, "... employees must eat at properties which accept credit cards and will use the credit card in all situations, unless the property doesn't accept anything but cash."

If all employee submitted receipts were honest, this would be a stupid policy, as logically a burger joint or other fast food place which operates on cash would be cheaper than almost all of the places which accept credit cards. The company would end up paying more than they had to.

It's best to push the envelope on this one. If you are skipping lunch and turning in the tear off receipts for a few bucks, I'd do it until someone questions it.

Then you might say, "Gee, I know the policy, but the cheapest places I can find to eat which take credit cards would've cost me at least ten bucks for lunch. This diner was only four and a half. Do you really want me to spend twice as much of the company's money for lunch than I have to?"

If your boss or the company replies that you must use the charge card, they've just handed you carte blanche to cheat. Now you can turn in higher dollar, bogus credit card receipts. Also, if you document the conversation, you have what amounts to a "get out of jail free" card.

If at some later date, they question your expenses, you can point to your documentation and say, "I wanted to save you folks money, but no, you told me to spend twice as much as I had to. I'm confused. Am I really supposed to hold down expenses or blow unnecessary money to comply with the policy?"

If your company accepts the tear-off receipt for restaurants, then you are home free. If they require the charge slip, you'll just have to get more creative.

Airline Tickets

I am going to cover airline tickets in detail later in the book. The airline is a good way to add big dollars to your expense report and get it into your pockets. To do it, you need to find out what is required when you submit your report.

The greatest inventions for cheating on expenses were E-tickets, which do not have the typical receipt. The employee gets an itinerary and an invoice copy. There is no real ticket. You show up at the airport at what you hope is the proper time and place. They take your name and print you a boarding pass.

The E-ticket created a very easy method to pad expense reports. Check to see if your employer needs the invoice copy, itinerary, or the used boarding passes. I'll tell you why this is important later in the book.

If your company's travel agent still issues real tickets, you again must find out if they pay from the receipt which is typically the last page in the packet, from the itinerary, or from the used boarding pass.

It also makes a difference strategically, as to whether they bill your personal credit card, or the company's accounts.

Hotels and Rental Cars

Again, some companies require you to submit the actual charge card receipt. Some pay from an invoice or folio printed by a hotel or rental agency. It's important to know which one the company requires for payment.

Later in the book, we'll look at the difference it makes for hotels, but either way, if you spend a little time and pre-planning, hotels can be a lucrative way to pad your expense reports in virtually untraceable ways.

Also later in the book, we'll look at rental car methods. They are the hardest ones to pad directly. Indirectly, they are a good source of a few bucks here and there for parking and fuel. To be able to cash in for bigger dollars with rental car agencies, you will have to know which receipt is acceptable by your company.

Taxi Cabs & Limousines

You can pad a ton of money in this area, all of it depending upon what documentation your company will accept.

Don't let the term limousine fool you. In many cities this is a big ugly van, crammed with as many people as a shoe horn will permit. In other cities, one notably Indianapolis, the true limousine services keep their cars busy during the day doing airport runs. In Indy, they are often cheaper than traditional taxis and there is a certain amount of ego stroking which comes with climbing out of a stretch limo at a hotel.

Either way, in most all cities taxi cab receipts are actually the backs of business cards, and usually very cheaply and crudely printed business cards. If for some unknown reason you can't get a few "extra" receipts from a cabbie, you could certainly print them yourself.

Some companies will accept these as proof, and so you can obviously fill in whatever amounts you want. Other companies will only accept them if they are filled in and signed by the cabbie. For a few extra bucks on the tip, cabbies will fill in whatever number you ask.

If you don't have to have a signed and filled in receipt from the cabbie, a few extra bucks on the tip will get you a handful of blank receipts. Cabbies are true entrepreneurs. A few bucks cash for a few pieces of paper, is a good deal for them as well.

Unfortunately, some employers require you to use a charge card for these taxi trips. The cabbies hate them, because they have to do special procedures to process the card and their tips as reported on the card are reported to the IRS. It is hard to get help from any cabbie on charge cards.

Just be sure you know or have tested which kinds of receipts your company will accept.

General Comments

There is a difference between what the expense policy says and what actually happens when bills are paid. The only way you know, is to test the system.

Remember I told you your boss really doesn't feel like spending a lot of time reading your reports, and their secretary is even less likely to care. Generally, if everything is backed with some kind of receipt and if everything totals correctly, your boss will sign it.

The accounts payable department pays hundreds or even thousands of bills everyday. They have even less incentive to "audit" your expense report. They will usually recheck to see if everything totals and foots, and if your boss signed it. If it looks right and is signed by your boss, they pay it.

Your boss and the accounts payable people don't always know the documentation policy very well either, so test the waters. A little bit at a time, submit one or two tear-off receipts instead of the charge slips the policy requires. If they get through, try some more. The more quantity and frequency of receipts you get by them, the better track history you have for covering any future discoveries.

Let's say one day your boss is being nosy and finds a tear off receipt. When they remind you that policy requires something else, you simply reply, "Well, I've been turning those in for months now. You've never said anything and A/P has been paying them. I just thought it was okay."

In most cases, the boss will acquiesce. The last thing they want to admit to A/P is that they have been letting improper receipts get by. The boss will usually say, "Well, if A/P is paying them, then it must be okay. I'm not going to over-rule them."

Even if everyone says to stop submitting them, you can apologize and promise to not do it again. You still managed to get all of the others through and paid. Then you can wait another couple of months and start running one or two through again until someone else notices.

The first rule of padding your expenses, is the same first rule as paying less taxes to the IRS. It is:
"If you volunteer to follow the rules, you'll never get anything. If they ever want it back, they'll ask for it."

Chapter Two

Legitimate Perks To Remember

There are several lucrative benefits which come to you as a side benefit of having an expense account. Before I go into the unethical ways to gain profits from your expenses, I wanted to discuss with you a variety of ways to maximize your benefits from those methods which are legal.

Even in this area, there are companies out there who are trying to figure out some way to steal all your bonus points and airline mileage away from you and put them into their pockets. Can a company benefit from your airline miles and such? You bet they can! Can the executives in the company benefit from your airline miles? Absolutely!

If you remember earlier in the book, I told you the executives will turn on you in a heartbeat if they can benefit their own positions. This is a confirmation.

The company gets limited benefits from this policy, but the executives can directly benefit from the free tickets, profit sharing from reduced expenses, and upgrades to first class accommodations.

In fact, if your company books a big convention, they will specifically block the individual flyers from using their own frequent flyer numbers. They will strike a deal with an airline to consolidate the flights in return for a number of free tickets.

I've arranged conventions for the company and I can say in those cases, the free tickets were not used for attendees. All those free tickets were issued to the president of the company, for use on future "business" trips. If the true purpose was to save the company money, why weren't the free tickets used for some of the convention-goers?

The government, via the IRS, has even tried to figure out some way to make you pay taxes on your frequent flyer points and other programs. Besides it being difficult to measure and value, the court challenges to this will take decades, as it directly impacts personal constitutional rights of the public.

Let's take a look at each of the major categories available to you. I'll explain some ways to maximize your benefits and warn you of ways your company will try to prevent you from getting those perks.

Airlines

Every major airline has a frequent flyer program. Although they vary in how miles are compiled, tracked, and issued for flights, they all follow some similar rules. Their rules have to be similar. If one airline offered a significantly different and better program, the rest would have to follow suit or risk having all of their members jump ship.

Legally, the airlines deny any collusion in this area. They have to because it would violate anti-trust laws. That's what they claim, but a couple of years ago, one of the carriers raised the miles necessary to get free flights and lowered the minimum flight miles paid per segment. Within days, one at a time, all of the airlines changed their program rules. This is quite a coincidence.

Just in case you do not know, this is how these frequent flyer programs work. You join into a program. This almost always is at no charge. Every time you fly, you or your travel agent enters your account number on your ticket and you are credited automatically for the miles you fly.

Most programs give you a minimum of 500 miles for segments you fly which are less than that many miles. For a flight longer than 500 miles, they credit to your account the actual miles flown.

An interesting exception to watch out for, is this. Let's say you are on a flight which leaves Las Vegas for Memphis. Your plane stops in Houston, but you do not change planes. The airlines call this a continuation flight.

The airline will pay you the straight line distance from Las Vegas to Memphis, not the total miles of the two segments. If you do the geometry on this one, you'll see this can be a substantial loss of miles.

The airlines further incent you to monopolize your flying dollars, by setting "levels" in the program, at which you start to get better benefits. Let's make a fictitious airline called Princess Air.

In the mileage program for Princess Air, we credit you a point for every mile you fly up to 25,000 miles a year. At that point, we send you a new ID card and inform you that you are now a member of the Silver Club. As a silver flyer, you earn 1.5 points per mile, your own reservation number to call, and the ability to purchase low cost upgrades to First Class, which you can reserve 24 hours ahead of time.

Once you fly 50,000 miles in a year, we bump you to Gold Club. As a Gold Club member, you earn double points per mile flown, we send you some free upgrade coupons a few times a year, we allow you to book First Class upgrades 72 hours ahead of time, and you get free drinks on the flight.

Once you fly 100,000 miles, you achieve Platinum Status. As a Platinum flyer, we give you triple miles, free parking at the airport, and your own personal flight attendant on-board.

Okay, so I went a little too far, but the airlines will really add bonuses for you as you build more and more miles with them. So, if you want the maximum benefits from an airline program, you need to fly one carrier as much as you can. This is where your employer begins to cause you grief.

Your company will want you to fly the lowest fare regardless of the carrier. (Would you be surprised to know, that top executives are usually exempted from this policy?) You can protect yourself a little by signing up for EVERYONE's program. That way, no matter who they ask you to fly, you'll get some credit.

Another way to protect your points, is to offer flying Saturday nights to reduce the airfare. Your boss will love you. Flights Monday through Friday are much more expensive. They are often $500 more expensive. At these higher prices, the likelihood of there being a cheaper fare on another airline than your primary choice is higher. If you fly an airline that still offers even lower fares with a Saturday night stay, fly them.

Remember, Saturday night stays end at midnight at your originating airport. On west coast to east coast flights, you can take a "red eye" flight leaving at 11:30 pm and arrive early Sunday morning. Your employer likes the reduced fare, and you can get a free day of sightseeing in the town you are visiting. If you can learn to sleep on the flight, it is a great deal.

Another way to avoid having to fly an alternate carrier, is to fly a complicated route. In other words, you would find a lot of price competition on flights from Chicago to Los Angeles. You will not find too many discount bidding wars for a flight that goes from New York to Detroit for a couple of days, then to Denver for a day, and then back to New York. Often on these more complicated routings, it is always cheaper to have you fly on one carrrier for the entire trip.

On some airlines, there are hidden perks which they do not advertise. On some carriers, once you reach a certain mileage level, usually about 50,000 miles, you begin the next year at your old bonus level and do not have to start over. This means as much as 50,000 extra miles the next year in bonus points.

On some carriers, the higher level members can bump lower ranking flyers for upgrades, stand-by flights, and even flight reservations. On the actual flight in coach class, the higher ranked flyers get to board first and sit up front, closer to the door, and the center seats are blocked until the last minute to maximize the chances you will be sitting two in a three person aisle. Basically, the airlines do many things to reward those who build miles with them.

Airlines allow you to turn your miles in for a variety of items. You can get free tickets to virtually anywhere in the world. Prime destinations such as Hawaii and Europe take a premium number of points. On some carriers, if you have to fly from New York to Hawaii, you have to use points to buy a continental United States ticket and then buy another ticket for the continental United States to Hawaii, so be careful.

Besides tickets, some carriers allow you to use your points for upgrades for yourself and any other person flying with you. Some allow you to use points to buy memberships in their airline clubs, where you get better access to phones, free snacks, televisions, and more pleasing surroundings.

From time to time, the airlines will hold auctions where you can bid points for exotic trips and vacations. These can be great deals.

In addition, when you redeem miles for tickets, you will usually receive other coupons for upgrades or free days with the airline's rental car and hotel partners.

Some employers do have an expense policy which would allow you to use your frequent flyer miles for business travel and then the company pays you for the ticket. This policy seems good for you, as you get cash for free miles. You have to be careful though, as they seldom reimburse you the full price the ticket is actually worth.

The employer usually pays a percentage (50% or 75%) of the lowest fare available. You must balance the money you receive from helping the company with what a free ticket on a personal vacation might be worth to you. Later in the book, I'll show you another way to turn those miles into cash - at top dollar!

Airline frequent flyer miles are one of the best benefits a traveling business person can utilize. You need to do your best to protect those miles from being lost by or to your employer. You also need to do the best to maximize your bonus points.

One of the best ways to "parlay" your points with the airlines is to tie it in with hotel programs, rental car programs, and charge cards.

Airline Sponsored Charge Cards

Every major airline has a credit card affiliate, it's usually with one large bank, which pays you miles for all of your charges. If you are the type of person who pays off their credit card balances every month, they are a great source of bonus miles with the airlines. If you normally carry a balance on your cards, the deal isn't that good, as these cards usually have a much higher percentage rate charge than you can get with other bank cards.

By getting one of these cards, every dollar you charge for tickets, car rentals, hotels, meals, and even your new pair of tennis shoes, earns you miles with the airline. Typically the rate is one mile per dollar. Some premium cards like Diner's Club will pay multiples of two or four miles per dollar.

Some of these cards have annual fees which will be waived or reduced by the company if you are a higher ranking frequent flyer. Some of these program cards have annual limits to the miles you can accrue, unless you attain the higher program status. Nonetheless, the more you use the card, the more miles you collect.

The biggest problem with these cards is your employer not allowing you to use the card for travel related matters. Why would they do that? Money to them, of course!

Often an employer will make "available" to their employees a "corporate card" from one of the majors like American Express or Diner's Club. It put corporate in parentheses, as the only thing the corporation does is put their name on the card with you. The corporation does not guarantee the card in any way at all.

There are true corporate cards, where a company pays the bills directly, but only the top executives will get one. (See how it continues to differ?) The balance of the employees will get the other "corporate card" for use in their travels.

The company works a deal with say Diner's Club, where Diner's Club agrees to waive their membership fee for individuals. In return, the company agrees to write a policy which forces employees to exclusively use that card while traveling. This assures the charge card supplier with as much volume as possible.

You are still personally responsible for all of the charges and paying the monthly statements. If your personal credit is bad, you may not be able to qualify for the card. If you default on a payment, it will be your personal credit which is affected, not the employer.

What's in it for me? Not much. If you pay an additional fee, you might get some of the bonus miles credited to your account, but some card companies will not provide mileage credit for major airlines like United or American. So, if you're happy with miles for flyiing secondary carriers, it's okay.

What's in it for my company? A lot. Credit card companies charge a fee to the airlines, hotels, and such of between 2 and 4 percent on all charges to the card. More volume means more income to the charge card company. In most corporate programs, your employer gets a rebate from the card company. They more or less "split" the fees. For a company with ten million dollars in travel, a one percent rebate is still $100,000.

The best thing you can do, if your employer has one of these policy programs, is to still try and use your personal airline credit card as much as possible. The policy usually says you must use the corporate card or risk the company refusing to pay the expense.

Nice threat, but I'd like to see the sympathy an employer would get in court if an employee had to eat a large expense and then had to sue the employer to get it paid. For the most part, the policy threat is used like the IRS uses the threat of an audit. The chances of it actually happening is slim, but then the mere threat of it happening is enough to keep most people honest and following the rules.

Your best bet, is to use a corporate card wherever you have no choice, i.e. with the company mandated travel agent, and use your own card everywhere else until they tell you to stop. The corporate card will most likely be American Express or Diner's Club. Like the television commercials state, there are still a lot of places which accept Mastercard and Visa, which is more than likely what your airline card is anyway; but they do not accept American Express.

A little known program through some major credit card companies is a restaurant rebate program. These usually cost you an annual fee of $25 or so to join, but if you do a fair amount of business entertainment, the benefits to you could add up quickly.

In these programs, your charges at "member" restaurants is tracked. When you sign up, they give you a list of restaurants all over the world which belong to the program. At the end of the month, whatever you've spent at these selected restaurants will be totaled, and you will get a check for as much as 20% of the total bill.

This is a great deal if you can pull it off. You get airline mile credit and 20% cash rebated to you, for the expenses paid 100% by your employer.

Hotel Point Programs

Many of the major chains like Hilton, Hyatt, Marriott, and Holiday Inn, have tie-in programs with the airlines. In these programs, if you arrive in a city on say an American Airlines flight, you can give them your airline account number and they will credit you with 500 or 1000 miles.

Keep your eyes and ears open, as sometimes they run promotions where you get double or triple miles for a certain number of night stays, or by staying in a specific hotel in a city.

The hotels seldom ask for a boarding pass or ticket as proof, so even if you drove your car or flew in on a different airline, show your airline membership card and ask for credit. Most of the time, you'll get it.

Aside from these direct tie-in types of programs, many of the chains run their own point programs. These come in several forms with varying benefits, but if your company allows you to pick your hotel within certain dollar guidelines, aligning yourself with a particular hotel chain can reap pretty large benefits.

Some hotels give you a point or two for every dollar you spend. These points can then be used to "buy" products or services from a catalog they publish. These products can range from a fancy windshield ice scraper to large screen televisions and even around-the-world trips.

Some hotels allow you to redeem your points for free nights of stay or upgrades to better rooms. These can be very useful to you in planning vacations on your off time.

Some hotels have programs where they don't count the dollars, but offer you a free night's stay after ten or twelve nights in their chain. These night stays don't have to be at one location nor on consecutive nights. You can collect these all over the country, all year long. Some chains even give you the flexibility to convert these into airline miles instead of taking their coupon for a free night's stay.

In addition to these direct benefits, many chains allow you to build points and attain club levels like the airlines do. Your "gold" status may earn you a free breakfast and a paper that the average person does not get. Your "platinum" status may upgrade you to suites at regular room rates when available.

The way points compound on business trips will be discussed later, but getting airline mileage points from the hotel for your stay, paid for with the charge card which pays you airline miles, helps build points quickly.

Rental Car Point Programs

Generally, the rental car companies will limit themselves to the tie-in type of program where they will credit your airline mileage account with 500 or 1000 miles if arrive on that airline's flight.

The major rental car companies participate in most every airline's program, so chances are you will be able to get credit with whatever carrier you flew. If you want credit with a specific carrier, you should try the same thing you would with a hotel.

The rental car counter clerks seldom ask to see the ticket stub, so just have handy a flight number from your airline of choice (available by reading monitors in the airport) which arrived at a time near yours, and give it to the clerk. Ask for credit. You will most likely get it.

Something else to keep in mind with the car rental agencies, is your company's "national" contract, if they have one. These usually allow you to rent a variety of car sizes with rates which vary by only a dollar or two per day from the cheapest rate.

This is handy for two reasons. First, sometimes the rental company will pay premium points, double or triple, if you rent a specific class of car. Ask, either when reserving or picking up the car, if they are running any "manager specials" at this location.

The second reason is simply comfort for you. Typically there are two types of paperwork on a car rental - the contract and the invoice. The contract is the paperwork you typically carry with you as you drive the car. You get your invoice, usually a computer print out and charge slip receipt, when you return the car.

The contract shows the class of car you rented in some code form, number or letter. The invoices hardly ever show the type of car rented. Rental car rates vary drastically around the country, so unless your boss sees the contract, they have no idea whether you rented a $50 a day, sub-compact GEO Metro in New York or a $40 a day, high-performance Mustang in Indianapolis.

By knowing the type of receipts acceptable for submission on your expense report, you could rent a better car, get bonus points, and enjoy the good life. Think about it.

Parlaying Points for Maximum Benefit

Assuming you have the freedom to pick and choose, who you fly and where you stay, let's see how you can work a business trip to maximize your points and airline miles. Let's say that you belong to an airline frequent flyer plan and you've booked enough miles that you've made the club level which pays you double miles.

You must take a four day business trip from New York to the Los Angeles area. The actual office you are visiting is halfway between LAX and Orange County airports. The airfare is the same to LAX or Orange County, $1500 round trip.

You do some checking, by calling different rental companies on their 800 numbers, and find out a rental company is running a promotion at the Orange County airport on Mustang convertibles. You get the mid-size car rate of $40 a day plus triple airline miles.

You do some more checking and find out that a major hotel near the airport is paying double miles and double hotel program points.

You pay for the trip on your airline credit card, which earns you airline miles. During your trip, you must host two dinners for ten people each. On this trip, you could end up with credit card charges which total something like this:

Airline tickets	$1500
Rental Car ($40 x 4 days + taxes)	$ 200
Hotel ($80 x 4 days + taxes)	$ 400
Two Hosted Dinners (10 people x $30)	$ 600
Meals and incidentals	$ 100
Total charges	$2800

When you total up your frequent flyer miles for this trip you could have totals like this:

Airline Mileage (2500 miles each way)	5000
Airline Bonus for Club Status	5000
Charge Card Point Mileage	2800
Rental Mileage (500 x triple)	1500
Hotel Mileage (500 x double)	1000
Total Miles	15,300

So, on one business trip, you've gained more than 15,000 miles on your airline mileage account. In most programs, free tickets are 25,000 miles, so you are more than 60% toward getting a free trip.

In addition, if you held all your dinners at the restaurant which is part of your credit card company's rebate program, they will be sending you a check for 20% or $120 for the meals. You also will get any of the benefits your hotel program points will buy.

All of these are benefits cost you nothing but a little planning time, and were graciously paid for by your employer.

Additional Benefits to Consider

Before I leave this chapter for the greener grounds of padding your expense report, I thought I'd remind you of what the ultimate benefit of having an expense account can mean - FREE vacations to exotic places.

Collecting all of these points and coupons over the course of the year, pay off big when vacation time comes around. Free miles for flights, free hotel nights in upgraded resorts, free car rentals, and discounts to attractions are just the beginning.

Just this year, I took a trip to Hawaii for a week. Using airline miles, my spouse and I flew first class across the country and then to Hawaii. Total value of the tickets if I had been forced to purchase them, $9000.

Using some airline miles, plus hotel points, we stayed in an oceanfront suite at a Hyatt resort. Total value of the room if I had paid for it, $2625.

I used some car rental coupons to rent a sporty convertible. Total value if I had paid for it, $275.

I used coupons and connections for discounted meals, a day cruise, and a helicopter ride. The total cost reduction of these totaled about $300.

To make a long story short, by being smart all year long, watching where I stayed and counting every airline mile I could grab, I got a virtually free, week-long vacation in paradise worth more than $12,000.

Since you didn't pay for this with your own hard-earned money, the vacation is a pre-tax raise of more than $20,000.

I rest my case!

Chapter Three

How to Make Money on Airlines

If you are going to make big money in padding your expense report, it makes sense to begin with the largest dollar items available. Airline tickets are one of the biggest travel expenses, so we'll begin there.

Most people look at airline tickets and wonder how they could possibly get money back on expense reports. The number one factor in making money is how closely your boss tracks your travels.

For most of us, when we're out of the office in the field, no one calls or checks up on us. They usually use the voicemail for communication and the chances of someone actually calling the branch office that we're visiting is slim.

In fact, in a couple of jobs I've held, hanging around the office, no matter how productive you were, raised the suspicions of the bosses. They'd ask, "What does that person do?" On the other hand, if I was "in the field", they thought I was really on top of things.

I could literally tell them I was flying to the Reno office for a couple of days and hang out in the casinos. As long as they didn't call the office and I checked my voicemail, I returned to a normal office who believed I was working hard. If they did call the office, I could just claim I was taken ill and just forgot to tell the branch.

How do you make money on your expenses when the airlines control the tickets? A lot of it depends upon the types of receipts your company requires you to use in backing up your expenses.

What you can get away with, also depends on who books your flight. You can do many more things if you can use your own travel agent or if you can book tickets on your personal computer. If you are locked into a travel agent within your office, you are a little bit limited, but not shutout.

Another variable in what you can get away with, is what type of ticketing you receive. The E-ticket, where you don't actually get a ticket, but show up at an airline counter to check in for your flight using your name, are the best. E-tickets open ways to rip off your employer in ways we never had before and they never thought existed.

The E-ticket was invented by airlines to reduce their costs. They claim it is beneficial to you as a flyer, but no one has been able to explain it to me in a way that makes sense. A number of people have tried, but the simple truth is it saves the airlines cost and they want to do it. If they all get together and force us to use them, what can we do?

Your travel agent loves them, as they never have to deliver the actual tickets to you. They can either email or fax you a copy of the schedule. This saves them a lot of money in postage and express mail charges.

I'd like to first start by defining some items which I will need to talk about later.

Itinerary - An itinerary is a piece of paper which lists schedule of travel, confirmation numbers, telephone numbers, and any other pertinent travel information.

Receipt - There are two types of receipts. There is the receipt you receive from the travel agent which is most often called your E-ticket, and then there may be a separate charge card receipt.

Invoice - When using E-tickets, your receipt may actually be called an invoice copy.

Boarding Pass - When you check in for your flight, they will often print you a boarding pass, which is what the old "real ticket" looked like, and it has your actual seat assignment for the flight.

Some employers pay from the actual E-ticket or invoice, while some employers want those plus your itinerary. You need to figure out the ones your employer wants. The reasons will become clear a little bit later.

It is also necessary for you to understand a little something about airline ticket pricing schemes. There's an infinite variety of ticket options and rules governing your tickets which can impact you and your ability to make money on your expenses.

<u>Unrestricted Fares</u> - Most business travel takes place on what is called a full fare or unrestricted fare ticket basis. Most business travel is Monday through Friday and often booked at the last minute, so they are unable to take advantage of discount fares. Statistics have shown that less than 50% of the flyers today are business flyers, but they generate 80% of the revenues for airlines, because they are paying for very expensive tickets. These tickets are totally refundable and totally changeable.

<u>Restricted Fares</u> - These tickets cost a little less, and have some restrictions about when you can make changes, what those changes cost, and whether they can be refunded or credited to another ticket.

<u>Discount Fares</u> - It used to be if you could stay over on a Saturday night and buy your tickets seven, fourteen, or twenty-one days in advance, you could get

a very cheap ticket. Now it refers to the cheapest ticket you can buy. Usually the tickets have many restrictions. They can not be changed without paying a fee and they can not be refunded. In many cases, for a modest fee, they can be credited toward another ticket within a year.

Back-to-back Booking - this used to be a way that if you have to book at the last minute, you could still manage to get a discount ticket. A full fare ticket from Chicago to Los Angeles may cost $1400 round trip. But if you were tricky, you can buy two discount tickets which total less than the full fare. You do this booking your outbound flight from Chicago and a return two weeks in the future; and then book the other round-trip ticket starting from Los Angeles on your correct return date and a return two weeks in the future. You threw away the unused back halves of each of those tickets and they still total less than full fare. (If you were really good, you could get your employer to pay for these two tickets and schedule the other halves to give you a free week-end round trip on another date. Play with the dates to see what I'm saying.)

Other than these general descriptions, it is nearly impossible to understand airline pricing. Back when Denver opened their new airport, the city of Colorado Springs was running promotions to encourage people to use their airport. A round-trip ticket from Denver to Los Angeles, was $400 more expensive than tickets which started and ended in Colorado Springs, but were connected through Denver. Does extra flights for less money make sense?

Changing Discount Tickets

The airlines officially tell you that these tickets are non-changeable and non-refundable, but there are things you can do. You can cancel your reservation on a discounted ticket and the ticket will "pend" inside most airline computers for a year. You can then credit them toward another ticket, for a fee. The costs run between $35 and $60 per change, depending upon the airline.

The same thing can be done to protect mileage points due to expire. If you have some account miles due to expire, you book a free trip ticket to wherever and whenever. After a few days, call them and cancel the reservation. In most cases, those tickets will stay active for an additional year without a charge.

With some of the newer frequent flyer account programs, the carrier will re-credit your account for the points. Some carriers' computers can credit the account with the original expiration dates, so they'd still die. If that is your carrier, you may try this trick. For most programs, you need to redeem the tickets by expiration dates, but they can be used on tickets as much as a year from that day.

Accepting Overbooked Offers

Airlines will routinely overbook flights, betting that a certain percentage of people will cancel or change their flight, thus freeing up the needed seats. Airlines track this carefully over time on very popular routes. They actually are pretty good "bookies" when it comes to this.

Every once in a while, they make mistakes and the overbooking results in too many people trying to get on the same flight. The airline will then make an announcement over the loudspeaker, asking for some volunteers to give up their seat in return for some money, coupons, or meals, plus a seat on a later flight.

If you are flexible in your schedule and you can volunteer, this can work out well for you. As with all situations, there are a few things you need to know. The airline wants to spend as little as possible to get you to give up your seat.

This first thing you and all of the other potential volunteers need to know, is this is really an auction. The airline has to get volunteers or deny someone getting on the plane, so you have quite a bit of leverage.

The beginning bid from the airline will usually be something like a $100 discount coupon for use on future airline tickets, plus a ticket on the next flight that's going to your destination. If no one bites at this level, the airline will up the offer. I have seen the airline offer a first class ticket on a later flight, plus two tickets for free travel anywhere in the United States, and dinner coupons while waiting for your flight.

If the airline has a later flight, and it is also overbooked, they might offer you a ticket on another carrier. If you want the mileage credit, you are better off waiting for a later flight on the same carrier. If you accept the flight on another airline and they are not your carrier of choice, you will not get mileage credit for the flight. Your credit will be on the flight they shift you to, if you have a frequent flyer number with them.

The airlines can and will offer different things. They have several kinds of coupons giving discounts on future flights. Some coupons limit you to 10% of the ticket price you are buying and some are just like cash without limits.

The airline can offer you free flight coupons for travel anywhere in the United States, good for a year or two. They can also offer you meals at the airport, or even off-site restaurants. If your delay requires you to stay overnight, they will provide a hotel and allowances for meals, and even toiletry kits, if you ask for them.

When getting the later flight, you should always ask for an upgrade to first class. If they have the room, it costs them nothing, so most of the time you can get it. Ask politely and sincerely. Flight attendants and gate workers hate pushy and obnoxious people, and have delightful ways of getting even with them. If you don't want to end up in the last row, back in the corner near a noisy engine, seated between two screaming kids, be nice when asking.

Making Money With Discount Coupons

There are many ways for you to acquire discount coupons for airline travel. Banks offer them when you open new accounts. The airlines will send them to you sometimes as part of your frequent flyer status changes. Rental car companies and hotels will give them to you for using them.

The point is, airlines love them, as most of the coupons are limited to say $25 on a flight of $300 or more. The airline still got $275 or more for the ticket. A ten percent discount on a ticket is still 90% in their pocket.

For you though, you could use these coupons for easy money in your pocket. If your employer accepts either the hard copy ticket receipt or the itinerary, and you are allowed to use your own travel agent, you can use the coupons to help pay for your ticket. Your receipt will show the total price of the ticket, not how much you actually had to pay out of pocket.

If your employer requires you to also show the credit card receipt, you'll have to be more creative. In this scenario, you'd pay for the ticket at full-price, get a receipt, and then ask the travel agent to credit a coupon as a separate transaction afterwards.

This same process can be used to get full credit for free tickets bought with frequent flyer miles. Pay for a refundable ticket on your credit card. Keep your credit card receipt and the itinerary to turn in on your expense report. Refund the ticket and then re-book it using your frequent flyer miles. Cross-country tickets without advance purchase can easily run $1800, so if you can do it on your frequent flyer miles, it's a hefty increase in your bank account.

Of course, most of these go out the window if your company has an in-house travel agency. In that case, I'd suggest you find out which agent is the least intelligent and try to talk them into creative accounting. You may even want to bribe someone. Travel agents do not make big bucks, and one might be willing to stretch the company rules to help both of you.

Double-Booking Tickets for Profit

Almost all airlines have computer systems which allow you to book as many tickets on a flight as you want. The reason for this is common names. There could legitimately be five John Smith's on a flight. So if you really wanted to, you could reserve every seat on a flight with John Doe.

If you were to book three tickets on an flight, over a period of a couple of weeks, you would likely have three different fares. It becomes fairly obvious that once you knew you were going to be making a trip, you could reserve and book a ticket. Then you wait a week before your flight and book another ticket at what is most likely a higher rate.

When you get closer to the flight day, cancel the higher priced, fully refundable ticket, and fly on your discount ticket. You turn in the higher priced receipts on your expense report.

If you use your own travel agent, they can do the refund. If you have a company based travel agent, you can still send the ticket to the airline or ask for a refund at the airport counter. This will avoid tipping off your company as to what you are doing.

E-tickets make this whole process easier, as the only thing you get for proof, is the invoice from the travel agent, which is usually faxed or emailed to you. Even if you have an in-house travel agent, E-tickets are simple. Once they fax you a piece a paper showing the price and itinerary of the ticket, they can't retract it. Even if they did demand it back, you photocopy the fax, or re-print the email, and it still works.

On full fare tickets and some advance tickets, you can play a waiting game to see if your carrier runs a bargain fare deal before you actually take the flight.

Reserve the refundable fare and watch the fares. If the carrier runs a fare war rate, you cancel the higher fare ticket (keep the receipt for your expense report) and repurchase the lower fare ticket and fly on it.

The E-ticket receipting has made expense report padding so easy, a child could do it.

Flying Less and Making More Money

When you book a trip for business and it involves more than one city, it will most likely be a full fare ticket or at least a fully refundable discount ticket. When you get in a situation like this, you can change your plans, chopping off the last segment or layover, and you might get a refund for the difference.

Say you're flying from Chicago to Phoenix, and connecting through Denver on Monday. On Tuesday, you fly to Los Angeles. On Wednesday, you planned to fly from Los Angeles to Denver for a meeting, flying to Chicago Thursday morning. The act of "breaking" the flight in Denver adds to the cost of the ticket, when it's compared to a Wednesday flight from Los Angeles to Chicago, connecting in Denver.

If you call the airline and cancel the flight "break" in Denver, flying through Denver directly to Chicago on Wednesday, you may reduce the ticket by as much as $300. Full fare tickets are not front-end loaded like discount tickets, so generally all segments will carry a decent price tag. When you show up at the counter Wednesday morning, the airline will credit your credit card for the difference in the fares.

By calling the airline before you even ticket the flights, you can see if this method works for your flight. Ask them, "What would happen if I..." You may even routinely add one day's trip on your tickets, knowing you are going to cancel the last segment for profit.

Most of us could do this without explaining to our boss what we did the extra last day. I'd just fly home Wednesday and take the next day off as if I were flying back as planned. I would get a free day off, plus the money in my pocket. On my expense report, I'd use the E-ticket receipt and itinerary from the original booking and routing.

If your boss found out, you could just claim to be feeling ill and decided to fly home instead of throwing up in a hotel room somewhere. You'd say you forgot to tell the appropriate person about a sick day Thursday. If you don't like the illness route, you could claim that business plans had changed. Either way, your boss is unlikely to think about the fact you got money back on the ticket.

Should I Really Be Doing This?

Airline tickets can generate big extra dollars on your expense reports, but they require effort on your part, extensive planning, and considerably more risk than some of the other techniques.

If someone puts two and two together, it is hard to defend your actions as anything but deliberate. You should think long and hard about doing any of these. If you have any second thoughts at all, you should not do them. If you think there is any audit trail at all, you should avoid them.

If your boss gets serious, they can always ask the airlines to print out a listing of what flights you actually took and when. If the travel agent is in-house, they can easily compare those flights against the original routing and see what changes you made and if there were any changes in the airfare.

On the other hand, if you are looking to put a few hundred dollars per expense report in your pocket, airline tickets are the easiest way to do it.

One Last Review On E-tickets

This is best summed up by saying:
"Buy and refund full fares, using the receipt for your expense report. Buy and fly discount fares, throwing away the receipt afterwards."

Airline fares change daily and a flight in the morning can be twice the fare of another flight in the afternoon. There's no way a supervisor (unless they fly the same routes often) can know what the best fares are. As long as your refundable fare is reasonable, they most likely will never question it. If they do, you say, "I tried to find the lowest fare, but when I booked this flight it was the lowest fare I could find."

Chapter Four

How to Make Money on Hotels

Never let a travel agent book hotel reservations without some guidelines from you. This is the area of the reservation process they know the least about and care about the least. If you leave the choice to them, they will mess it up.

Travel agents live on commissions paid to them by the hotels and airlines for making reservations. These amount to a maximum of 10%. How much time do you think they'll spend hunting, for the seven dollars your one night hotel room booking garners them?

If your company has an in-house travel agent, they will pick the first hotel which pops up on the screen which fits the company's dollar limit policy. There are a number of problems with this.

First, you have no idea where you'll end up. You might be twenty miles from your meeting place, because the travel agent simply looks at the city name. In a city like Denver, you'll have suburb cities like Englewood, which meander through, in and out of other suburbs which were formed later.

There's a Holiday Inn ten miles out of the city, in the countryside, east of Denver near a general aviation airport. It's a great place to stay, but it is thirty miles away from the main sections of Englewood, and both show up in the travel agent's computer as Englewood.

The second thing that will happen is they'll book you in a Day's Inn, basic hotel because they found it first on the list, when in fact there's also a Hilton at the same or lower rate. Your Hilton mileage credits would be lost, unless the travel agent knows your preferences.

You can save yourself a lot of time and bonus points the next time you stay at one of your favorite hotels, by picking up a directory of their locations and keeping it handy at your office. When you get ready to travel to a city, see if any of them are in the town. If they are, tell your travel agent you'd like to try these first. They'd love to save themselves from hunting through the whole list of hotels, if they can find one of your choices within the company budget guidelines.

Check the flyers you receive in the mail from the hotels and airlines. Many times there are special deals like triple points for staying at specific hotels in a city.

The travel agent may tell you they can't book you into the hotel of your choice because the computer says their rates exceed the limit set by the company's expense policy. Don't give up. Call the hotel directly and talk to the reservation clerk there. Many times if you ask, they are running local special rates which can get you within the company's guidelines.

If you don't get the answer you'd like from the reservation clerk, ask to speak to the manager. Tell them, "I would prefer to stay at your hotel rather than over at Hotel XYZ like my company wants, but to do so, you'll have to get me the same rate." If the manager knows the hotel is under booked, they'll gladly give you the better rate to fill a room.

You might not get it, but it's worth a phone call, particularly because the phone call is either on the hotel's 800 number or your company phone. It costs nothing to call, but can help you get the points you want.

Another thing to find out, before you arrive or immediately upon your arrival, is if the hotel is running their own private frequent stay program. There's a Hilton near the airport in Pittsburgh, which once ran a promotion, where every dollar you spent there gave you a point toward prizes.

It wasn't limited to the charges on your room rate only. It included catering, meeting rooms, and meals. I was doing a three day seminar for twenty-five people. By the time all the charges were totaled for the stay, I accrued 4,000 points. This got me a free color television set which I still have.

There was also a Holiday Inn in King of Prussia, Pennsylvania which ran a promotion where each night you stayed, gave you a point toward luggage, really nice luggage. Some hotels will even do programs which give you meals in their restaurant or drinks at the bar. It never hurts to ask.

Just as another aside, always ask if there are any free room upgrades available. Every hotel keeps a "slush pile" of expensive rooms not currently reserved. Often, just by asking, they will upgrade you for nothing extra. This will most often happen if you are spending just one night. I know this doesn't seem to make sense, but let me tell you why they do this.

When the hotel gets down to just a few rooms left and someone calls at the last minute, they can easily sell the lower priced rooms. Most last minute callers confronted with having to pay big dollars for a suite will most likely call elsewhere to find a better rate. So, if the hotel can upgrade you to the more expensive room and keep a few lower priced rooms for those last minute reservations, they can and will do it.

How to Get Blank Hotel Receipts

Getting blank receipts from hotels is fairly easy to do. Many are generic, in that they have the hotel chain's logo and home office address and such on it, but the local address and phone number is printed on the receipt by their computer when you check out.

Most company's will accept the receipt from the hotel, without the back up of your actual charge card receipt. The reason for this, is most hotel computers will print at the bottom of the receipt, "Paid In Full" or it will print, "Paid with Credit Card #123456".

If this satisfies your boss and accounts payable office, you can literally write your own receipts on your home computer or a typewriter, if you have some blank receipt paper.

The easiest way to get the real blank forms, is to simply ask for it. When you are checking in or out, mention to the clerk, "Hey, I really like the layout of your invoice paper. I'm sure my boss would like to see if the format would work for our company. May I have a few sheets to take back with me?" Most clerks will just hand them over to you.

If they can't or won't do that, there is another way. Many times, while loading their printer, the hotel wastes a few sheets aligning the forms. The clerks sometimes use these for scratch paper. You could too. What you do, is act a bit confused at the counter and then ask for one of the sheets to take a few notes.

Failing the above methods, there is always the old stand by method of going through the trash. The evening crew usually is the one who collects the trash and replaces the plastic bags in the office trash bins. They often stack the bags outside of the back door leading to the office, so a janitor can pick them up in the morning.

No one watches them well. This is unfortunate, as this is probably the most frequent method criminals use to get used charge card slips so they can use your number. I don't condone it. For some strange reason, I don't see anything morally wrong with ripping off my company through expense reports, but using someone else's charge card number is not fair to fellow travelers.

If you need blank receipt forms from the hotel, you could "borrow" one bag long enough to rummage through it for the paper you want.

How to Get the Hotel to Print Fake Receipts

I know it sounds crazy, but if you know how, you can get the hotel to print faked or inflated receipts for you, and they won't even know they are doing it.

Every time you make a reservation, the hotel or the national reservation service will quote you a rate and enter it into your reservation record. The clerks have literally hundreds of rates available to quote. There are rates for the AARP, the AAA, IBM, and even the NBA. There are rates for seniors, juniors, and probably even sophomores. The point is, there are many rates besides the one you were quoted, available for the asking.

If you know you are entitled to let's say a AAA discount because you belong to the auto club, don't tell them when you make the reservation. Let them book you in at the normal "rack" rate. Before you arrive, call the hotel and ask someone what the AAA rate is. Note their name, the date you inquired, and the rate.

If you have an in-house travel agent, don't tell them about your special discount opportunities. Let them book your hotel at their corporate rate and then call the hotel to see if your discount is better, and then try this method.

When you check in, the hotel will usually circle the rate on the reservation card and ask you to initial it. They want you to do this, so there is no dispute when you check out as to what rate you were going to be charged, which is exactly what it is you want to do.

The clerks are not always observant once they hand you the card, especially if they are busy. First, try not initialing the rate. If they don't catch it, you're home free. If they catch it and ask you again to initial it, go ahead and initial it, but in a completely different way than you normally would.

The key to this trick is the fact that the clerk who checked you in, late in the evening one night, is not the same clerk who checks you out the next morning. What you want to do in the morning, is get them to print a copy of your bill for examination. In almost all hotels, this will be your receipt if there are no objections.

When they hand you the bill, you dispute the rate. You are armed with so much information at this point, they will not be able to argue it, although they will try. You can tell them, "Hey, this was supposed to be the AAA rate. I talked to so-and-so, on this date, and they quoted this rate."

That statement alone, backed with so much fact, will normally be enough to get them to re-print you the corrected and lower priced receipt. Your original, higher priced receipt goes in your pocket to be submitted with your expense report. Ten dollars per day less for a five night stay will allow you to get an extra $50 plus taxes from your employer.

If the clerk tries to enforce the ,"...you initialed the rate on the card when you checked in..." argument, you can show them you did not initial the card, if in fact you didn't. If you did with the unusual initialing, you can say, "Someone else must have initialed this, because I sure didn't. This is how I initial things."

If you cause enough commotion, calmly and coolly, you will almost always get the re-print. If they still refuse, it is no skin off of your nose, because the company will be reimbursing you for the full price. You just won't be able to get the extra cash... TODAY!

The fight is still not over if the hotel shuts you out. You can still write their corporate office and claim they misrepresented their rate, that they were rude and uncooperative, and whatever it takes to make them sound like ogres. A hotel's corporate office will almost always send you a refund.

Sometimes, you can innocently end up doing this two rate switch. This happens when they fail to get the correct rate on the reservation card and you're checking in very late. The manager is obviously not on duty, so if you have a rate dispute, there is usually nothing that can be done until the next day.

Ask the clerk to note on the registration card that the rate is disputed. When you check out, let them print the incorrect bill, and only then ask them to resolve the dispute and re-print the bill.

Another minor way of getting a higher priced bill to submit, involves the fifty to seventy-five cent charges which are often added per phone call on your bill. This is supposed to be for local calls, but some hotels charge this for every outgoing call, even 800 numbers. If you do a lot of calls, this can be five or ten bucks per day.

When you check out and after they have printed your receipt, ask to have these charges removed from your bill. This is totally at their whim, but if you are firm and forceful, you can get them waived. The newly re-printed bill will be lower and you turn in the higher one for your expense report.

Some other minor benefits which hotels provide for you involve room-service. Once again, this has everything to do with receipts and being firm.

The first benefit is room service usually arrives with an invoice which also has a tear off receipt at the bottom. Sometimes these receipts have the hotel logo on them. That's okay, it will still work as a receipt on another meal. If the receipt actually has the hotel's fancy restaurant logo on it, that's perfect.

Sign the receipt over to your room bill, so you pay for it as an entry on your hotel receipt, an entry for use on your expense report. The tear-off receipt is now a blank one you can use some other time and place for proof of a meal purchased.

The other benefit takes nerve. If your meal is very late in arriving or they deliver the wrong meal, call the kitchen manager and demand a refund for the meal. Even if the food is great, you could call and complain and get it free or reduced. The charge shouldn't hit your hotel bill as it happened in the same billing period, but you still have the tear-off receipt to turn in later as an expense.

How far you want to take these techniques is up to you and your conscience.

Chapter Five

How to Make Money on Rental Cars

This most likely will be the shortest chapter in the book, as making money on rental cars with your expense report is the most difficult trick to do. Part of this has to do with the sophistication of the computer systems most of the major rental companies currently use.

Almost every rental agency uses the remote printing computer hand-sets to complete your billing when you return a rental car. This combined with the highly automated rental procedures of the reservation clubs, which preprint your contract, leaves little or no room for error or human intervention.

To make serious money on a rental car requires more out right dishonesty and effort on your part. The risks associated with this, and the time wasted to pull them off, may not be worth it.

I'm not quite sure how rental car agencies got so tight with their procedures in this area, because if you look at their overall operation, their procedures in all of the other areas are terrible.

Most of you who travel much at all, should join one or all of the rental car agencies reservation clubs. They all work about the same. You fill out a profile which the company keeps in their computer and they issue you an identification number.

When you reserve a car, they access your record, and preprint a rental contract at the time of your arrival. The profile tells them the class of car you want, and it tells them what special contract pricing agreements are in effect, and what credit card to charge for the rental.

In theory, you arrive at the airport and go directly to the bus which takes you to the rental lot. When you get there, your name is on a board which tells you where your car is parked. Your car is ready with the contract usually hanging on the rearview mirror. In the winter, they sometimes have the car warmed up and running for you.

I have terrible luck with these programs. I often travel twenty weeks a year and make stops in two or three cities each trip, so I rent a lot of cars. In certain cities, like Chicago, I can guarantee my car is never ready. If it is, it is either the wrong car, it's out of gas, a tire is flat, or the battery is dead.

Since I've got the room, let me warn you of a few diabolical tricks the rental car agencies do to get more money out of you. If you are reading this book, you may not care if the company pays more, but for your personal rentals, you'll want to know about these.

Most of the major agencies offer some sort of gasoline option. They try to scare you into buying this option by warning you, "If you return the car with less than a full tank, we'll charge you $50 a gallon to fill it."

I know this is an exaggeration, but they don't make you wait for them to fill your tank and charge you for the missing gas. They charge you based on the miles driven or a prorated calculation based on the amount showing on the fuel gauge. They sometimes charge you as much as 20 cents per mile driven. In a compact car, this can be more than $5 a gallon.

They tell you that if you pre-pay for a full tank of gas, usually at a rate they claim is a dime or two below local prices, you can bring the car back with the tank empty and they will not charge you. What they don't tell you, is they also will not refund the money if you bring the car back half full or full. Unless you're really good or like taking risks, you're going to bring the car back with a decent amount of gas still left in the tank. You paid for gas you did not use, and that's free money to them.

Another trick they like to do, is talk you into an upgrade at your cost. This happens in facilities which still make you go to the counter to rent a car. It most likely occurs in smaller cities, but I have had someone try this on me in Houston. When you check in, they'll say they can upgrade you to the next level of car for only a couple of dollars a day.

Again, this is more free money to them. They're counting on the fact you don't care if you spend a few more of the company's dollars. In fact, the clerks are usually given a bonus for every upgrade they can sell.

The primary difficulty with using the rental car to generate expense report revenue, is that your receipt is printed at the absolute end of your transaction, after several checkpoints have occurred. It's hard to claim you didn't have the car you had, when you are showing up with it to check in for the receipt. Besides, when there is a problem and a receipt must be changed, they are obsessive about getting your copy of the incorrect receipt back from you.

It can be done but it is going to slow you up, both checking in and out, as the only real way to do it will require human intervention. I would suggest it isn't worth your time, as the human factor working in the car rental world is really poor. They are slow, they are inflexible, and they do not want to help. Their whole system is designed to make human to human contact an exception to the rule.

How to Get What You Can

One area where you might get away with receipt tampering, involves coupons for discounts. This will generally only work on those which have fixed dollar amounts off of the rental. Sometimes you can get away with using the buy one day, get one day free coupons. To use them, you are going to have to be firm and maybe even obnoxious.

You return your car like normal, get your receipt, and then walk into the office where you would pick up the bus for the trip back to the airport. If you try to hand the coupon to the person checking you in at the car, they'll defer printing you a receipt and refer you inside for help. You need them to print you a receipt BEFORE they send you to the office.

You have to walk in, hand them your coupon and claim there's been an error. You say, "I told them when I made the reservation that I had this coupon and they were supposed to mark my record for the contract. They told me I'd have to hand the coupon in when I returned the car. Now I'm told I can't use it."

If you push hard enough, you can get them to credit your charge card for the amount of the coupon and possibly let you keep the receipt from the original printout. This takes a lot of time and energy, which can be completely wasted if they take the receipt.

The only real option you have is to completely fake a receipt using adding machine tape through your dot-matrix printer or on a typewriter. You've got to be really good to do it. You start with an actual receipt and copy the format. There's a ton of information encoded on the receipt and you've got to be very accurate with your information if you want it to look legitimate.

What Other Areas Can I Use to Get Money

Fortunately, there are other areas of rental car use which can be used for your expense report, which are easier to fake or exaggerate. One of those is a gasoline receipt.

For most of us, we can expense the gasoline used in the rental car. There is no standard format for the gasoline stations around the country, as far as receipts are concerned. If you use the automatic charge card islands at the gas station, you'll lock yourself out, but if you pay inside, you've got a lot of flexibility.

Some older gas stations leave a book or stack of blank receipts near the cash register for you to take if you need one. Gas station attendants really hate to fill out receipts, especially if you only put a dollar or two of gas in the car.

Some gas stations hide the forms, but they will hand-write the amount on what is supposed to be a credit card receipt. If they hand-write a dollar or two, adding a one on front of it makes it eleven or twelve dollars. Make sure you turn in the carbon copy, as they will not be able to trace the two different colors of ink that way. If you aren't comfortable with that much of a discrepancy, one dollar can become seven quite easily, particularly on the carbon copy.

Another thing to think about with gas stations is to watch for the receipts of other people who did not take them with them. This is very easy on the self-serve credit card islands, as a lot of people take their receipt and then throw it in the trash. A quick look in the bin might get you a computer printed receipt for several dollars more than you are paying. These are wonderful because they will carry the name of the gas station, maybe the city name, and a time/date stamp which matches your travel plans.

Some gas stations use just a regular cash register receipt for gas as well as groceries and beer. Look around the counter and see if anyone who bought a case of beer, left the receipt behind. You can use it for your expense report.

The only possible problem you have in this area pops up if your rental car receipt shows the number of miles driven. If you turn in a gasoline receipt for ten gallons worth of gas and you drove fifteen miles, you could have a problem. This is fairly easy to cover, by claiming the return clerk entered the wrong mileage by dropping a hundred miles in the calculation.

Within reason, there are a number of legitimate reasons why there may be a sizable gap between the mileage driven and gallons bought. Many times, the person who rented the car before you will drive twenty miles and return the car without filling up the tank, claiming they did. You get a car which is already down a gallon or two.

The same thing can happen to you, if you rent from a facility who intentionally "shorts" the tank by a gallon while preparing the car for rental. Some rental locations do this. If they save themselves a gallon per rental, times a thousand rentals a day, it adds up nicely for them.

Finally, car mileage can vary from the thirty plus miles per gallon on a GEO Metro, to the fifteen miles per gallon of a Lincoln Continental. So, unless your rental receipt has a car type mentioned, some variation is expected.

Parking is another area which you may be able to pad by picking up stray receipts or adding digits to the amount. If you are entitled to claim a reasonable amount of parking on your expense report, you can pick up a few bucks here and there.

Some parking garages provide only the barest of receipts, a simple cash register tape which only shows the amount tended. These make it easy, as they seldom have dates or times on them, so you can look around for others sitting around with higher amounts.

Those parking facilities who use the computer generated receipts can be faked like rental car receipts if you want to reproduce them on your computer or on a typewriter. The correct types of paper including the chemical carbon copy types of paper can be found at the office supply store.

One other area which is open to the discretion of your company or boss, involves cash used for parking meters or tolls. You can't visit areas of the country like Chicago or Pennsylvania without dealing with toll booths on the roadways. These almost always operate on a cash only basis and getting receipts from some is darned near impossible.

If your company or boss allows you to submit an amount without receipts for tolls and coin operated parking, then you can obviously inflate the amounts above what you actually spent.

Car Related Expenses

This is the best place I can think of to deal with two issues. Both are related to mileage reimbursement for the business use of your personal car. One is being paid by your employer for using your car on business, and the other is using a rental car instead of using your personal car, for business.

The IRS allows you to be reimbursed by your employer a certain amount per mile for the business use of your personal car. Company policies seldom pay the full IRS amount, but they come close. The IRS amount changes from year to year sometimes. Depending upon how your personal taxes are handled, you may be able to reclaim the difference on your taxes.

For the sake of this argument, let's assume your employer reimburses you 25 cents per mile, when you use your car for business. The first obvious fact, is you can easily add miles without your employer finding out. There are always multiples of routes between two points, as well as the need for little side trips and errands once you are at your destination.

If you travel only a 1000 miles total for employer a year, you still could probably add another 200 miles without raising any suspicion. This extra mileage would give you another $50. It isn't big dollars, but it is free money. If you use your car more than that, say 5000 miles per year, you could easily hide another 1000 miles for a raise of $250.

Now let's look at another scenario. Let's say your boss wants you to drive to a sales meeting in another town 360 miles away. With the round trip, incidental trips, and errands, you could probably rack up nearly 1000 miles for the trip. If you actually drive 750 and your car gets 30 miles per gallon, you'd spend about $32 on gas, whether you drive your car or a rental car.

You will burn the gas and put these extra miles on your car, causing wear and tear which depreciates your vehicle. If the meeting is a three day trip, you could try renting a car and not telling your boss. You could probably rent a car for less than $40 a day, so your rental would total $120.

For the 1000 miles you are turning in to your employer, you will be paid $250. You will save the wear and tear on your car, plus pocket $130. Your boss doesn't care whose car you drive, only that you are there for the meeting. The next time you have to take a sizable drive for your employer, do the math and see if you can leave your personal car at home.

Chapter Six

Making Money on Meals & Entertainment

If there ever was an area on an expense report custom made for abuse; meals and entertainment is the one. No other area of the expense report has so little control by outside agencies and so much control in your hands. You are in total control of the process.

You select where you eat. You can control who you take out for lunch and where you go. You decide if you are going to eat one, two, or three meals per day. Only you control the facts needed to back your claims for reimbursement on your expense report.

The really sweet thing about this area of business expense, is you can do it with the advanced knowledge and permission of the boss. Getting prior approval makes things so much easier to hide or inflate. Go to your boss and say, "You know, it might be a good idea to take the purchasing agent from ABC Bowling Supply out to dinner. I think I'll do that next week. Should I invite her husband?"

Your boss, will most likely agree, and tell you to invite the spouse. Now you have a blank check to do whatever you want. You could turn in receipts as if you took the two of them and your spouse to dinner and pocket the whole meal. You may want to take only the purchasing agent to dinner, but turn in a receipt with four people's worth of meals. You could take your own love interest to a fancy restaurant, and turn the receipt in as if it were four people at a reasonable restaurant.

The combinations may be endless here, but the point is obvious, as long as your boss is not with you, you can make up whatever story you need.

Methods Involving Your Personal Meals

You are entitled to eat while you are on the road. Your employer may pay you as a per diem for meals or allow you to expense actual charges. Your employer may set dollar limits per meal or a daily total limit for all meals. Whatever they do, you have the latitude to make a lot of money.

If you are on a per diem, you need to manage things to get as many free or cheap meals as possible so you can pocket the difference. The thing to consider is the hotel where you stay on your trip.

Many of the hotel chains offer a free breakfast as part of your room rate. These are usually a continental breakfast, meaning you get rolls, donuts, juice and some coffee. At some properties, the breakfast can include toaster waffles, cereals, fruit, and even some breakfast meats. If the hotel has a substantial breakfast, you may be able to skip lunch by eating a big breakfast. You could take a couple pieces of fruit with you, or a granola bar or two, to eat for lunch.

If you can talk someone else into buying you lunch, you save your per diem money. You might even get desperate enough to agree to lunch with a vendor or sales rep. It's better to listen to a sales pitch you don't want to hear than to pay for a lunch out of your pocket.

In addition to breakfast, some hotels offer a "happy hour" with hors d'oeuvres in the evening. Some have enough of a spread, that it easily could be made into a meal. Stocking up on cocktail weinies, tacos, or vegetables with dip can minimize the need for a dinner. If you eat a big breakfast, bring along some fruit for lunch, and eat a big plate of snacks, you could get by without spending any of your per diem for meals.

Another thing to consider, if you are on a per diem, is to stay at a hotel which has a mini-kitchen or full kitchen in your room. If you have a refrigerator and microwave, you could easily cook your own meals. Cooking for yourself can be very cheap and more healthy than eating in restaurants. Anything you save versus your per diem, is money in your bank account.

If you get to use actual receipts, you can get away with murder. The first trick is getting receipts. Learn to collect them. If you can't collect them, stop by the local office supply store and get a package of receipts with the tear off bottoms. The thing you have to be careful with on the tear off receipts, is they come with serial numbers printed on them. Don't be silly enough to use three receipts in consecutive order on the same report.

You can easily collect a huge stockpile of these blank receipts, as they can be found all over the place. Every time you pass a restaurant at a hotel, walk up to the host or hostess and say, "I ate here yesterday and forgot to get a receipt, can I have one off of the bottom of a receipt." They'll always give you one or two.

If you see receipts sitting from other patrons, snatch them up for use by you later. If you see extra receipts sitting next to the cash register, pick them up. When you pay with a credit card for a meal, the original order form used by the waiter probably had a tear off receipt on it. Keep the receipt for later and use the credit card receipt, or use the tear off receipt to report a higher priced meal than what you ate and paid for.

One of my favorite tricks in this area can best be exampled by a trip through O'Hare airport in Chicago. If you eat at one of the snack bars and go through the check out line, the clerk will hand you a receipt. If you lower your eyes a foot or two, you'll see a pile of other receipts left behind by other patrons, at the base of the cash register.

If you grab a handful and go through them, you'll inevitably find receipts which are for amounts larger than what you spent. You keep the most expensive one you find, and turn it in on your expense report. The beauty of this is the receipt has the name of the airport, the date, and the time. You are entitled to eat while on the road. You're legitimately at the same place, at the same time, on the same date as you are expected to be. It becomes the perfect inflated receipt.

Some employers will not accept tear off receipt, and will write policies to restrict their use. In an earlier chapter I covered how to get around this with your boss, but there are other ways to get your employer to accept the tear off receipt more easily.

Sometimes employers will feel more comfortable if a restaurant employee signed the front of the tear off receipt. You could obviously forge fake signatures if you wanted, but it would be safer to ask a friend or a spouse to fill in the amount, sign ,and date the receipt for you. That way, there is no way the signature looks like yours and if you're asked if you filled it out, you can honestly say, "No."

If your employer allows you to turn in the actual receipts up to let's say $40 per day, you could do the following. Eat the continental breakfast at the hotel and turn in $4.76 on a tear off receipt for breakfast. Skip lunch and turn in $9.88 on another tear off receipt. Eat the happy hour snacks at the hotel that night and turn in another receipt for the $23.86 "dinner" you didn't eat.

You'll collect $38.50 for meals for which you did not eat or pay. Do this each day on a five day trip and pocket an extra $192.50 for the trip. Do this twenty weeks a year and take home an extra $3850. That's a pre-tax pay raise of over $6400.

To be safe, you should probably vary the amounts significantly and maybe even skip a meal or two to make it look different. You can still protect your total dollar amount, by turning in a breakfast for $9, skip lunch, and turn in a dinner of $28. You get the variance in your pattern which helps confuse your boss, and you still get close to the dollar limit for the day.

One last thing to think about. Let's say you are going on a business trip to Las Vegas or New Orleans. The company is paying for your airfare, rental car, and hotel. If you use some of your frequent flyer miles, a spouse or friend could accompany you on the trip for free. This set-up is especially nice if you volunteer to fly on a Sunday to save the company on the airfare.

In Las Vegas, the two of you could easily feast on buffet breakfasts and prime rib dinners and still be within your daily dollar limits for your own personal meals. You simply turn the receipt in as if it was your meal alone. In many other towns, you could still eat at modest restaurants within those limits. Either way, the company would be paying for your personal vacation.

Cashing In On Lunch and Dinner With Others

If you have the clearance to buy lunch and/or dinner for others, you significantly expand the amount of room you have to add expenses to your pocketbook.

Your boss is <u>not</u> going to call someone you claim to have taken to lunch to see if you really did. There are few things your boss could do which would be more stupid than that. If it is a customer; your boss, your company, and you would lose all credibility.

You might as well kiss off any chance of ever doing business with that person or firm again. Even if it was legitimate and you had taken them to lunch, the fact your boss called to check, destroys all credibility your company has with that customer. I don't think any boss is that stupid.

If my boss would ever ask one of my clients if I took them to lunch or dinner, I'd go through the roof. I would quit on the spot and tell my boss I'm suing the company. Even if the suspicion were justified, nothing undermines your reputation with a client more, than having your boss "checking up" on you. No judge is going to be sympathetic with a boss who did that.

Now that we have this on the table, it naturally follows you can get away with a reasonable amount of fictitious entertainment. Just be sure you don't claim to have taken Bob Smith to lunch on the same day your boss happens to be golfing with Bob Smith. That one is a little too obvious.

Saying you took someone to lunch or dinner, when you didn't even buy lunch or dinner yourself, is doubly good for your finances. You pocket two meals worth of cash from your expense report. Saying you wined and dined two other people is triply good for the bank account.

I'm getting ahead of myself here. Someone years ago told me something which makes infinite sense. They said, "When you're out on the road, you've got to eat. You might as well ask someone out for a business lunch, and eat for free."

That's a lesson I've never forgotten. If business routine includes the ability to take others to lunch, you can eat for free. Although this doesn't put money into your pocket, it saves you from spending your own money for lunch. If you would normally spend $5 on yourself for lunch and you'd do this 200 days a year, you save yourself $1000 by buying someone else lunch as a business expense.

Now the next step in escalating your income is to have the business lunch, but with someone else who is going to turn it on their expense report. Obviously this works best with someone from another company. They expense your meal, but on your expense report you submit a receipt as if you had bought the lunch. You ate lunch for free, saving your own money, plus the company will reimburse you for both lunches you did not buy. That's like getting triple pay.

Another really slick way of pocketing a lot of cash, is to arrange for a fairly large group of people, let's say ten, to meet at a restaurant after work for someone's birthday or anniversary. You make it clear to everyone that they are on their own, but that you will "run a tab" to make it convenient for the group, on your credit card. At the end of the evening, everyone pays you their share in cash. You have a legitimate receipt to use on your expense report. Even if the gathering is a conservative ten dollars a head, you got $100 cash from them, and you'll collect $110 when you turn in the receipt.

Always remember the program on your charge card, where participating restaurants rebate as much as 20% of the meal to you in a check each month. Not only can you collect twice for the meal, but you'll get another twenty bucks through the mail.

Another thing to remember is although it isn't money in your pocket, meals paid for by the company saves you from spending your own hard earned cash. For instance, how does your boss know the business dinner you bought last night was a client and not a love interest of yours? Taking a boyfriend or girlfriend to dinner at a first class restaurant can have other fringe benefits to you. It's that much better if the company is paying for the meal.

Golf, The Final Frontier

Lunches and dinners are not the only kind of business entertainment companies will allow you to expense. Tickets to the theater, sporting events, or local festivals are often used as sales incentives. Taking your client golfing, hunting, fishing, or boating is common. Later in this chapter, I'll cover gifts in detail, but a lot of business is bought every year with corporate gifts to customers.

Those of you who do not golf, have no idea how many business opportunities have been lost to you. Whether or not you enjoy the sport, there are few other activities where you can get a business client, one on one as a virtually captive audience as you can during a five hour round of golf. An executive who will not give you five minutes in their office, will spend all day with you if you are "spanking the white ball" on the golf course at your expense.

I firmly believe the best business advice that a university can give to all its students is, "Go forth and develop a good short game." So much big business is conducted and deals finalized on the golf courses of the United States, that business schools should make golf a required subject in their curricula.

For you, the benefits of being a golfer with a job which allows you to expense golf outings, is absolutely wonderful. The first benefit is personal. If you can spend a day a week golfing for free at the company's expense, you getting a free day off relaxing in the sunshine doing something you love.

The second benefit can be financial savings, as in getting someone else to pay for your golf fees, maybe free golf balls and golf shirts with the company logo, and lunch at the snack shop. Golfing is not cheap. A decent golf outing for two can easily add up to $100. At prime golf courses, the kind the company's executives prefer to play, the same outing can run as much as $500. Even if you were playing by yourself once a week at a public course, getting the company to pay just your greens fees would personally save you $1500 a year.

A third benefit is the ability to play golf and pocket a lot of cash. Some clients, because of their company's rules, will insist on paying for their own golf fees. If you get to the golf course early and pre-pay the fees for both of you, you can get the client to pay you their share and still expense the entire outing on your expense report. If you want to really push it, you can claim to be golfing with someone or a group, when in fact you are golfing alone. You expense for a fictitious foursome when you have actually paid for one.

Golf seems to be an area where you can convince your boss to cheat on their expense report. If they are also a golfer, you can sometimes get your boss to agree to a golf course meeting. This has the benefit of the "bonding ritual", where you become golf buddies. Most companies will not allow co-workers to expense much of anything, especially golf outings. However, your boss may agree to have you pay for the round of golf and turn it in on your expense report as if YOU took out a client.

Why and how would your boss want to do this? It's simple actually. Most companies use an approval process called "one over one" for expense reports. I turn in an expense report and my boss is the only approval needed. If my boss turns in an expense report, their boss is the only approval needed. If my boss wants the two of us to go golfing without raising the suspicions of their boss, they make me pay for it and put it in on my expense report. The boss approves my expense report and no one else is the wiser.

This has double benefits for you. If your boss wants to pay for your golf so the two of you can talk about work, that's great for you. Better yet, you have evidence of your boss cheating on their expense report. It will become difficult for them to discipline you for an indiscretion, when you have proof of their cheating.

Aside from the actual outings, there are many other benefits to you. Companies love to give away golf balls with their logo on them. It's like free advertising lurking in woods, ponds and backyards all over America. Golf shirts, umbrellas, divot tools, towels, and even golf bags can be emblazoned with the company logo. Obviously meant to be gifts to clients, it is also necessary for you to have them to "show your company spirit" out on the course. These are all supplies you didn't have to buy with your own money.

Meals Are Not The Only Form of Entertainment

Tickets to local sports teams, professional if you live in a big city, are very popular with customers. To make the purchase worthwhile, it's necessary for you to go along to the game with the client. After all, you can not talk business with a customer unless you are there to speak.

Your boss may allow you to routinely buy these tickets for customers. If you do a lot of it, you may be able to convince your boss to let you expense season tickets, as they're always cheaper than buying individual tickets for every game.

You benefit in a number of ways if you can do this. First, you get to go to all of the games if you choose. Second, you aren't going to have a client available for every game, so you can treat friends and relatives at the company's expense. Third, if you decide not to go to the "most important game of the season", you could scalp your tickets for cash. Other benefits with season tickets are preferred parking, better seats, upgrades to even better seats as they become available each year, and preferred selection for buying tickets to play-off games.

Theater tickets are also great corporate gifts for clients. These can be bought as season tickets as well, at great "savings" to the company. If you live in a larger city where Broadway-type shows frequently visit, this can be expensive. If you go to see a traveling Broadway show, good seats easily cost $75 each. By getting the company to buy some tickets and accompanying the client to "make it worth our while", you can attend the show for free, maybe even including dinner before or after the show. If for some reason the client "cancels" on you, you could scalp the tickets for cash.

I could go on and on with examples, as the areas of meals and entertainment are the best and easiest way to cash in on your expense report. All other methods of cashing in, are variations on the ones I just gave you. In this area, the receipt requirements vary immensely and the ability to trace facts is severely limited.

Meetings, Conventions, and Seminars, Oh My!

If you are ever involved with planning seminars and conventions for your company, a huge new arena of exploitation is available for you to use and abuse. Typical positions for which these areas are available are sales, marketing, management, and even secretaries and administrative assistants. Anyone who has to buy gifts, prizes, supplies and those promotional materials for the conventions, can cash in on these functions.

If you are one of the planners for a large seminar, your boss has handed you the ability to leverage the awarding of huge chunks of business, like hotel rooms and catering, to the highest bidder. Actually, your boss is looking for the lowest bidders for the services. You are looking for the highest bidder for yourself.

If you are negotiating a deal with hotels to hold a seminar in their facility, which will have dozens or even hundreds of attendees, you hold the purse strings on thousands, maybe hundreds of thousands of dollars of business. Shouldn't you get something from a hotel or convention center for turning the business their way?

You do not put yourself in a position of soliciting cash bribes from the vendors. Your boss would find that one out in a heartbeat and you'll get tossed out with the trash. However, you could "hint" to the vendors that you have certain "needs" which could be "incidentally" taken care of by those who are "appreciative" of the business we've done in the past.

What does that mean? When you're negotiating the deal and accepting bids, you be very specific with the vendors. Tell them your company policies are such that you can not accept gratuities, either in cash or gifts for directing business their way.

However, you can mention relationships you've had with vendors, in the past, who in appreciation for the business you've conducted with them, surprised you with gifts at Christmas time or your birthday. Those considerate people have a "special place" in your heart.

Let me be specific. A hotel chain can give you some free dinners at little or no cost to themselves. They could give you certificates for free nights at any of their hotels, anywhere in the country. If the contract was large enough, the gifts might exceed these.

The important point, to avoid real problems with your company, is these gifts must "come from out of the blue" without an obvious connection. If it happens that way, you could go to your boss and show what they want to give you and ask, "I'm not really comfortable with this, but is it okay for me to use them?" Your boss will probably say yes. (Unless they want to take them from you and use them for their own.)

When your company rents a booth at a trade show, there is almost always a need to give away prizes in a raffle or drawing, in order to get people to stop by your booth. If you are the person asked to buy the prizes, why not buy something you'd like to have yourself?

Let's say you are sent out to buy "prizes" for the drawing. Your boss is unlikely to be one of the people populating the booth at the convention. Therefore, if you personally needed say, a camera, you could buy four prizes, keep one for yourself and raffle off the other three. If your boss sets a total dollar limit for the prizes, you can still arrange the distribution so that your personal selection is the most expensive.

If you want to add a safety margin to doing this, it would be easy to do. Buy the four prizes. Keep the one you want in your office and raffle off the other three at the convention. Turn in your expense report and wait for it to be paid. If they pay the report without incident and another thirty days go by, you're probably past any questions.

If on the other hand, someone puts two and two together and asks you about the extra prize, you can open your desk drawer and say, "I thought three prizes were enough to give away, so I thought we'd save this one for the next convention." No harm, no foul.

How far you push your luck in this area depends completely on how many people will have visibility to the prizes being awarded. If once the prizes are awarded, no one cares or knows who won, you can get away with quite a bit. If you have to publicly list or announce who won what, there's too much visibility and lasting evidence to risk too much.

Chapter Seven

What To Do If You Get Caught

As one of the final chapters, I found it necessary to discuss what to do if you get caught cheating on your expense report. Before I do this, I think we really should revisit the moral questions involved with whether or not you cheat.

As the first chapter of this book warned, if you want to go through life squeaky clean and never have anything that might blemish your record or conscience, do not do any of the things in this book.

The principles in this book are like a drug. The more you use them, the more you want to use them. Once you get away with five dollars, you'll want to try for fifty. You have to be very careful these ideas do not lead you into "harder" crimes against your employer.

Those of you who are fans of Star Wars movies will remember the discussions about the powers of the "force" and an admonishment to "beware the dark side" of the force. Specifically, the warning goes, "Beware the power of the dark side of the force. Once you start down that path, forever will it dominate your life." That's the way it is with padding your expense report. Once you start, there's little incentive to stop.

The more practical argument involved with whether or not you do this, is the possibility of losing your job. Some employers find absolutely no margin for error in such matters. Some employers will fire people if they take a box of ink pens home. They have a "no tolerance" policy in such matters. If you are found padding your expense report with even one breakfast or taxi cab receipt, you could be tossed out the door.

You have to be very careful to balance the value of your on-going employment with the extra bucks you are trying to get. I've seen it happen a dozen times in my career. I've seen a Vice President fired for accepting golf clubs from a vendor in exchange for awarding a small contract for parts. All the people in the company had the same reaction. They asked, "Why would he jeopardize a $100,000 a year job for a set of golf clubs?"

If you get caught padding your expense report, they could be asking, "Why'd they risk their reputation and job, for twenty dollars?" Before you try anything in this book, think long and hard. If you never cheat on your expense report, you have nothing to fear.

Now, let's look at the other side of reality. If the management wants you out the door, they will find something to pin it on. Making accusations against you on your expense report is an easy way to do it. It would be very easy for them to pull your last ten or twenty expense reports and go over it with a fine toothed comb. They can claim you added extra mileage. They can claim you turned in a breakfast receipt when you didn't. They can claim you did not take Betty Jones out to lunch when you said you did.

They could use this "mountain" of suspicious evidence to fire you, and your only recourse would be to prove them wrong in a court or at a wrongful firing hearing. By then, your reputation would be trashed. Even if you won the hearing or trial, you wouldn't be exactly welcome back where you work, nor would any future potential employers be thrilled about hiring you.

Either way, you could find yourself standing on the unemployment line. You could be squeaky clean on your expenses, and they could suspect you of cheating. You could cheat like hell, and they could suspect you of cheating. If you are going to pay the piper, shouldn't you at least dance?

I can not and will not make this moral decision for you. I can not and will not be held responsible for what happens to you if you get caught. I will try to give you some guidelines as to what you can say if someone questions your expense report.

Deny, Deny, Deny, and Then Deny Again

The first and foremost rule about cheating on anything is to deny it until proven wrong. Once they prove you wrong, then you can move to another excuse. Even if someone else claims to know you are wrong, deny it. What makes their recollections any better than yours? I've always subscribed to the advice of a friend, "If they don't have videotape, they've got nothing."

Let's say your boss questions the number of miles you drove your car on a trip. They say, "It's only 150 miles from Gary to Indianapolis. Why are you claiming 500 miles for the round trip?"

You could say, "I don't know why, I just know what my odometer read before I started the trip and what it read when I got back, and that's what I turned in. I didn't watch every mile I drove."

If they push and say, "That's ridiculous. It's only 150 miles down I-65. Where did the extra miles come from?"

Let's look at the facts. Gary and Indianapolis, Indiana, are fairly large cities. From the south side of Gary to the north side of Indianapolis may be 150 miles. On the other hand, if you are going from the north side of Gary, to the south side of Indianapolis, the distance may be as much as 200 miles. Depending on situations and how many side trips you had to make while in the city, you could easily explain the difference with facts.

Here are some more creative excuses you might try to explain mileage differences.

"There was a big accident on I-65 and the police detoured us out in the country I don't how many miles."

"I got into Indianapolis and made a wrong turn on I-465 and did almost a complete loop around the city before I knew I was wrong."

"I made a wrong turn downtown trying to find the hotel and with all of those one way streets, I thought I'd never get there."

"I went to the Holiday Inn near the airport and then I found out I was supposed to be in the one by the Pyramids. That means I back tracked twice."

"Someone told me about a really great restaurant to try and it was a lot further away than the person told me it was. What was I supposed to do?"

If someone questions your facts, just remember to deny, deny, deny, and then deny again.

Switch To Another Set of Facts

Always take advantage of the time differential between when you take the trip, complete the expense report, turn it in, and when someone may question the details. Whenever you fill out an expense report with bogus or exaggerated data, you should always think of an excuse before you do it.

If you claim to be eating lunch with someone, you need to be prepared with an alternative answer if your boss knows for a fact you didn't. If you claim a twenty dollar cab fare when your boss knows the office is one block from the airport, you need to have an alternative.

You've got days to think about every intentional error you put on the report, while your boss has only seconds to respond to your excuse. There is no excuse for not being ready to respond.

Let's say you turn in a receipt for dinner. The blank tear off receipt you used was from some major national restaurant chain. You picked it up on another trip and saved it for later use. Your boss shows you the entry on the expense report and says, "I've been to this town just recently, and I don't remember there being one of these restaurants in town. What's going on here?"

You could try the denial excuse and it might go away. A better technique would be to switch the facts. Tell your boss, "I know, but I ate at this one place and got into an argument with the staff there and stormed out without remembering to get a receipt. After I got back to my hotel, I realized my mistake and I had this receipt sitting around, so I thought I'd use it. The amount is correct and I knew that accounts payable would need some kind of receipt, so I used it. I didn't think anyone would mind as long as the amount was correct. Was that okay?"

Your boss will probably buy it and at the most, tell you not to do it again. This possibility should tell you to survey restaurants in the town you visit. I make it a point to drive around the town for a few minutes, noting the names of restaurants, major intersections, shopping centers, and things like big factories. If your boss gets too nosy about where you ate or where you went, you can talk intelligently about the town. If you are lucky, you may even be able to trip your boss up, by knowing more about the town than they do.

I Have No Idea How That Happened

Depending on what item your boss is questions, you may want to try an excuse of total amazement. This is actually a variation on the denial. The difference is you are not denying what the boss is accusing. You are simply acknowledging their accusation, but being amazed at what has happened.

It may be easier to understand what I'm saying, by substituting an exaggerated conversation. You could imagine yourself saying, "I know what you think you see here. I can't see it, but if what you say is true, then I have no idea how that happened."

Let's say you reserved a hotel room at $50 a night, but you did either a rate switch trick or faked a receipt which actually shows $75 a night. Now let's say your boss somehow got a hold of your itinerary and it shows the reserved amount. When they come to accuse you of doing something wrong, take the two pieces of paper in your hand and say, "I see the reservation form and the receipt from the hotel. They must have messed up. I know this looks strange, but I honestly have no idea how this happened. If you want, you can approve the report as is. I'll call the hotel and try to get them to credit me. If they do, I'll deduct it from a future report."

Your boss likely feels comforted and validated, and will approve the report, and move on to something else. The truth of the matter is, you will never call the hotel and never credit a future report. If the boss ever revisits this later, you simply say, "The hotel refused to do anything. So, I told them I will never stay there again and no one else in this company will either."

Challenge Your Boss As To Why They're Asking

Something I didn't tell you earlier in the book, about why your boss is not likely to check reports too closely, is a well kept secret. Your boss is probably also cheating on their expense report!

Within reason, your boss won't question expenses for concern someone will be alerted to a problem, audit everyone's expense reports and they'll be found out for padding their own reports. It is like the old proverb about throwing stones in glass houses.

From time to time, your boss may forget this, and in checking up on your expense report, you can remind them. You may even have a boss who believes it is okay to cheat on their own report, but they will not cut you any slack. That is an even better situation in which you should remind them.

Let me explain. You turn in a gasoline receipt for your rental car, where you've changed a two dollar slip into a twelve dollar slip by adding the extra one. If your boss comes in and accuses you of adding the one to cheat the company, you take the report and receipt in your hand and look at it for a minute or two.

You look at your boss with your best practiced indignant look and say, "I see what you are accusing me of. I'm not the kind of person who would ever have thought to try something like that. What made you think someone would do that? Have you ever done it?"

It sounds pretty strong, but the point is to divert attention away from the facts about the receipt. You need to get your boss off of accusing you about doing wrong, and get them defensive about accusing you of being a dishonest person at all.

The boss might get defensive, never wanting to admit why they thought of this cheating technique. They will also feel defensive for accusing you of cheating. Once you see they are on the defensive, you could go one step further and with a frustrated sigh, say, "Wow. I can't believe you thought I'd do something like that."

Chances are, your boss will drop the issue on the spot. They may even apologize for doubting you in the first place. If you listen closely, you may hear them say under their breath, "Sorry, but someone did this to me a long time ago, and I've been suspicious ever since."

If for some reason, it doesn't work, then you can switch over to another excuse mechanism. You may have to try the next one.

Offer To Take Back The Expense

If you press issues too hard, trying to legitimize a bogus expense, you run the risk of jeopardizing all of your future expense reports. This may be the time for a strategic retreat and offer to take the expense back.

The beauty of this trick, is you usually agree to give back nothing. If the receipt was totally fictitious, let's say for a meal you didn't eat, retracting the receipt costs you nothing. In exchange, you may completely shut down any future scrutiny. You need to weigh your position quickly and logically.

Let's go back to the receipt you turned in for the hotel rooms at $75 when they were actually only $50. If your boss is really digging in to the subject and you get the feeling they may call or write the hotel to get the duplicate records, you should regroup quickly.

Tell your boss, "You are right. It's my fault. I should have double checked the rate before I signed the bill. It isn't right for the company to pay the extra. I'll change my expense report and only charge the company for the $50 it should have been. I'll then deal with the hotel myself to get my own money back."

Your boss will likely respect your integrity and honesty, allow you make the changes, and let the issue drop. Monetarily you are out nothing, as the hotel room actually only cost you the fifty bucks. Strategically, you gained a great deal in lowering the suspicion level of your boss for future expense reports.

What To Do If You Get Caught Red Handed

No matter how good you are, you'll eventually make a mistake. No matter how careful you are, you will eventually forget some detail which will come back to haunt you. If you do this long enough and do it enough times, sooner or later, you're going to get caught.

It may take a long time. It depends upon how good you really are. I'm very, very good. If I weren't, I wouldn't be writing this book. I've never been caught, but I fully expect some day I will. When it happens, I will have to live with the consequences. If it happens to you, so must you.

One of the things I told you to do before trying any of the techniques in this book, is to weigh out the benefits of the extra income against the possible loss of your job. You can not have done it properly, unless you have resolved yourself to the fact that you feel it is worth it. So, if you get caught, admit to it and throw yourself on the mercy of the court.

Let's say you turn in a receipt for a dinner with the purchasing agent of one of your customers. On the same night, your boss is having dinner with the same person, at the same restaurant you ate at with your spouse, and your boss saw you there. You're busted!

When your boss asks you about this one, you'll probably be called into their office and the door will be closed. They may ask you some coy question like, "How did the dinner with Bill Wilson go the other night?"

If your boss asks you a specific question after you turned in an expense report, alarm bells should go off in your head. Don't answer the question with anything else but another question. Your only response is, "Why do you ask?"

When your boss confronts you with the facts, admit to the crime. Do not admit to having ever done it before, no matter how hard your boss may press you.

You simply say, "You got me. I knew you would, but I was short on money that week. I don't know why I did it. I gave in to temptation. I've never done it before, for fear of you catching me, and now that I've done it, I was right. I should have known better than to think I could get one by you. What do we do now?"

If you have a great reputation, you may only get yelled at and told not to do it again, as "they" will be watching you. If you're reputation is okay, but not that wonderful, you are probably going to be written up and it will follow you around the remainder of your career with this company. If you are a marginal employee, they'll use it as an excuse to kick you out the door. All companies consider the "theft of company assets" as a major offense, worthy of immediate dismissal.

So, you can see now why planning your excuses before making entries on your expense report is so darned important. If you can't explain something to yourself before, how can you easily explain it to your boss after?

The damage to your life and your career, can be devastating if you get caught red-handed. This is a game of strategy. There have been a number of times where I wanted to cheat, but my gut told me the risks of being caught were too high. Pick and choose wisely where you cheat.

Paraphrasing an old proverb, "Those in doubt, who choose to run away, live to cheat another day."

Chapter Eight

A Few Final Words

Congratulations. By now your head is swimming with sinister ideas about padding your expense report, and you're asking yourself, "Why didn't I think of that?"

I'll tell you something really scary. This is just the tip of the ice berg. I've only shared with you what I consider "basic" techniques. If this book is a success, I may consider sharing the more advanced ones.

Even though these are the basic techniques, let me take a few pages here to examine just how much the typical business person stands to benefit from business travel and expense reports.

For this discussion, we are going to assume this business traveler makes twenty trips per year which require airline travel. This person averages 3500 miles per round trip ticket. This is roughly between Chicago and Los Angeles round trip. The average cost of each round trip ticket will be $1000.

This business traveler is already at the point level in their frequent flyer club, where they are awarded double points per mile flown. We'll further assume they visit two cities per trip, with each trip being Monday through Friday. They will rent a car in each city for $45 a day for two days on each rental.

This person will be staying in hotels four nights each trip at an average of $80 per night. Because of the variance of towns and cities, and the availability of their hotel choice, this person will only get hotel partner miles with their airlines, at half of the stays.

This business person eats actual meals, and buys other meals as entertainment, at an average of $200 per trip. Half of these meals are purchased at restaurants which participate in their charge card rebate program.

Airline Points Earned By Traveling

The twenty trips on the airline, multiplied by the 3500 mile average trip, is 70,000 actual miles. This amount is doubled to 140,000 as this person belongs to the higher club level with the airline. In addition, these programs have "plateau" awards at 30, 40, and 50,000 miles. For this traveler, they gained a bonus of 40,000 miles for the plateaus. The total miles gained from the air travel for the year is 180,000 miles.

By using a rental car agency which is partnered with their airline frequent flyer program, this person earns 500 points per rental when they arrive on that airline's flight. On the twenty trips, they rent cars forty times. Multiplied by the 500 miles, they've earned a bonus of 20,000 miles.

This person stays at participating hotels only half of the time, as their hotel partner is not in every city, nor are they always available. So, with 500 miles per stay, this person adds 10,000 miles a year to their program balance.

In addition, they pay for these trips on their charge card which earns them miles on the airline. The charge card pays one point per dollar spent, so the year's charges could look like this:

Airline Tickets	$1000 x 20	$ 20,000
Car Rentals	$45 x 4 days x 20	$ 3,600
Hotel Room	$80 x 4 days x 20	$ 6,400
Meals & Misc	$200 x 20	$ 4,000
Personal Charges during the year		$ 6,000
	Total dollars charged	$ 40,000

Therefore, the total airline program miles earned for the year of traveling would be:

Airline Miles Flown	70,000
Airline Club Level Bonus	70,000
Airline Plateau Awards	40,000
Charge Card Partner Miles	40,000
Rental Car Partner Miles	20,000
Hotel Partner Miles	10,000
Total Airline Frequent Flyer Points	250,000

By parlaying points from all of the partners, you've earned a quarter of a million airline miles in one year, for flying only 70,000 actual miles. In most airline programs, 25,000 miles gets you a free ticket in the United States. Using the same $1000 average price for a ticket, as we used in the above examples, your frequent flyer points will buy you ten free trips with a total value of $10,000.

On most programs, 40,000 miles gets you a free first class ticket in the United States. That would be roughly six tickets per year. If the average first class airline ticket is $3000, then your frequent flyer points would be worth $18,000.

The harder things to value, are the additional coupons you get from the rental car and hotel partners who cooperate with the airlines. Rental car coupons can be used for free days of rental, usually on a buy one get one free basis, or upgrades to higher car rental classes for the entire rental. Hotel coupons might be for free nights, half-price nights, or upgrades, depending upon the hotel chain and the property at which you stay.

If you were only able to use them at the lowest redemption rate, and you used them all, they would be valued at a minimum of $1500. If you catch a few breaks and special deals, you may get as much as $3000.

Actual Dollars Earned On Your Expense Reports

For this example, I am going to assume someone being pretty aggressive at applying the principles in this book. This will by no means be the most you can get. I'm going to use the same traveler and circumstances we used in the airline miles example. This person will be pretty aggressive, but they won't be pushing it.

If you are someone who flies much more and wants to take more risks on every expense report, you can pocket substantially larger amounts of cash. The twenty trip per year traveler is probably closer to the average, and even with an average application of the padding principles, I think you'll be pleasantly surprised by the amount of money you can get.

One person stays at hotels with free breakfast and happy hour snacks, so they will be adding $30 per day in fictitious personal meals. They will be adding $20 per trip in inflated gasoline charges, tolls, and parking .

Using coupons, making schedule changes, and chopping stops from their airline tickets, this person will average $50 per ticket of inflated charges on an expense report. By twisting the arms and rules of the hotels in which they stay, this traveler will collect $5 per day in bogus or inflated expenses.

In addition, this traveler will expense fictitious or elevated charges for entertainment in the amount of $50 per trip. Finally, of the $4000 of personal meals and entertainment for which this traveler actually paid, half were at restaurants which rebate 20% through their charge card.

The last thing to consider is the cost savings to you of traveling. If you are on the road, you are not paying for meals you would normally eat at home. You are not incurring long distance phone charges. You are not running your water heater, furnace, television, stove, or other utility items as much as you would if you had been home.

When everything is totaled, this could easily be $25 a day you've saved. The money you did not have to spend on daily living expenses, is the same as extra cash in your pocket.

Never forget the incidental benefit of living for free on the company, when traveling on business.

The annual amount this employee will garner from their expense report in actual cash, could be:

Meals	$30 day x 4 days x 20 trip	$ 2400
Gas	$20 trip x 20 trip	$ 400
Airline	$50 trip x 20 trip	$1000
Hotel	$5 day x 4 days x 20 trip	$ 400
Entertain.	$50 trip x 20 trip	$ 1000
Rebate	20% x 50% x $4,00	$ 400
Personal	$25 day x 4 days x 20 trip	$ 2000

Total Cash Generated On Expense Reports $7,600

If you were this business traveler, you just gave yourself a cash raise of $7,600 over your normal take home pay. That's over $600 a month. Since it is cash or take home pay, you have to figure in the normal taxes. For most of us, this increase would have been over $12,500 before taxes. You have given yourself a raise of $1,000 a month without working any harder.

What's The Total Benefit?

Well, let's see. This person got a minimum of $10,000 in airline tickets by actively maximizing their frequent flyer program benefits. They got a minimum of $1500 in hotel and rental car benefits. They also got $7600 in hard cold cash. By my calculations, that is a minimum benefit of over $19,000.

Since this is take home or net money, absent of taxes, we need to figure out what the pre-tax amount would be. When you figure the average tax rate, you'll find these techniques can give you an effective personal raise of over $31,800.

What this means to you is a better, or at least a more affluent appearing lifestyle. If this person made $50,000 a year, they can live the lifestyle of someone making $80,000 a year. Any way you might choose to rationalize it. The benefits can be substantial.

Some Words Of Advice

I want to give you one final chance to reconsider whether you follow the advice in this book. It is illegal and unethical to cheat on your expense report. If you do get caught, you could get fired or sent to jail.

On the other hand, if your boss needs to reduce costs to make their profit numbers, guarantee their own bonus, or in any way get what they want, you could be a perfect employee and find yourself kicked out the door.

If you do get caught and they fire you, threaten to sue. Tell them, as part of the trial discovery, you are going to demand expense report copies from all the top executives to see if they cheated.

As a last piece of advice, "Don't worry, your boss is probably cheating on their expense report too."

One Final Postscript

There is no doubt you bought this book for the purpose of seeing how to pad your own expense report and get away with it. Chances are, if your boss saw this book, they bought it as well, for the very same reasons.

This book is a two way street and a two edged sword. It shows you how to cheat on your expenses, but it also informs you of ways your own employees are trying to cheat on their expense reports.

No one would buy a book called, "How To Catch Employees Who Cheat On Their Expense Reports...", but this book can and will be used in that way.

If this book becomes immensely popular and thousands of people read it, there will be an interesting little war going on in the business world. It'll be a war between those who read it against those who have not. I see myself as an arms supplier to both sides of the fight.

Friends who have previewed this book have asked me, "Don't you feel guilty encouraging all of those people to cheat on their expenses?"

My response is, "They already are!"

— **Employee X**